FUTURE

PROOF

JORDAN WYLIE MBE

ARMY CADETS NATIONAL AMBASSADOR

FUTURE

PROOF

HOW TO NAVIGATE YOUR LIFE
THROUGH VALUES

\B^b\

Biteback Publishing

First published in Great Britain in 2024 by
Biteback Publishing Ltd, London
Copyright © Jordan Wylie 2024

ISBN 978-1-78590-911-5

10 9 8 7 6 5 4 3 2 1

A CIP catalogue record for this book is available from the British Library.

Set in FreightText Pro, FreightSans Pro and Futura PT

Printed and bound in Great Britain by
CPI Group (UK) Ltd, Croydon CR0 4YY

FSC
www.fsc.org
MIX
Paper | Supporting
responsible forestry
FSC® C171272

*To the dreamers, the doers and the ones who dare to believe
in themselves, even when the world feels heavy.
This book is dedicated to you...*

CONTENTS

ABOUT THE AUTHOR

I'm Jordan Wylie MBE, former soldier in the British Army, extreme adventurer, charity fundraiser, TV personality and *Sunday Times* bestselling author.

Now I see that written down, it looks quite impressive. But growing up, nobody least of all me – thought I'd come to much. I grew up in Blackpool, on one of the largest council estates in England. At sixteen, I left school with no qualifications and a criminal record – not exactly the best start in life.

What turned my life around was learning how to live through values. I first learnt about values in the army – a lot more on that later – and since then I've tried to apply them to everything I do.

After leaving school, I served for ten years in the military, including operational tours of Iraq and Northern Ireland. I returned to education and gained my GCSEs, my A-levels, a bachelor's and a master's degree. I'm a champion for young people and have raised over £1 million for charities that help children access education in conflict and war zones around the world.

Since 2018, I've been a national ambassador for the Army Cadets, one of the largest youth organisations in the UK.

In 2023, I was awarded the Most Excellent Order of the British Empire (MBE) in His Majesty King Charles III's first honours list for voluntary services to charity and education both in the UK and overseas.

My proudest achievement, however, is being father to my teenage daughter, Evie.

INTRODUCTION

Welcome to *Future Proof*.

This book is for teenagers and young adults who are looking for guidance and inspiration to navigate our rapidly changing and complex world, or anyone who wants to be better prepared for their future. Whether you're just starting out in your career, wanting to make a change or simply looking for ways to improve your life, the lessons in this book will help you achieve your goals and live a much more fulfilling life.

These lessons are based on the values and standards of the Army Cadet Force (ACF), an organisation that's been shaping young minds for over 150 years.

The Army Cadets are one of the largest youth organisations in the United Kingdom, with over 100,000 members, including 60,000 cadets between the ages of twelve and eighteen. The organisation is built on the founding principles of *fun, friendship, action and adventure* and operates by the mantras 'Going Further' and 'Inspire to Achieve'.

I wrote this book because I strongly believe that you don't have to be a cadet or have any interest in joining the army, to benefit from the values and principles taught by both of these incredible organisations.

As you read through, you'll learn how to develop the skills, mindset and resilience you need to not just survive and cope through life but thrive in the face of uncertainty, adversity and change. You'll discover how to:

- Identify your values
- Set and achieve your goals
- Build strong relationships
- Implement the highest of standards in both your personal and professional lives

The ACF is a family that teaches young people the importance of values and standards. It instils in them a sense of purpose, pride, and a desire to serve their communities and help others from a young age, as well as learn skills that'll last a lifetime. As you read this book, you'll learn how to apply these same principles to your own life and reap the benefits of a healthy, happy and successful future.

You'll notice a series of activities for you to complete as you work your way through. I've called them **Everyday Adventures**. Don't panic, I'm not asking you to climb Mount Everest. These are easy, practical exercises that'll help you understand a bit more about yourself. Because I want you to think about adventure as a way of life and a way of thinking, not necessarily a far-flung destination.

Get ready to be inspired, encouraged and challenged as you embark on this journey to become *Future Proof*. I'll be with you every step of the way.

Jordan

GOING FURTHER

Anyone can change their life for the better

I've done it, not just once or twice but many times over.

As a lad, I'd often find myself in trouble both in and out of school. By my mid-teens, I'd made a name for myself, not only with my head teacher but the police and local authorities too.

Immature and easily influenced by others, I would skip school, get into fights and generally make poor decisions that, more often than not, would land me in a whole lot of trouble.

But the more trouble I made, and the more involved with the wrong crowd I became, the more I actually believed that this kind of behaviour was acceptable, even cool in some misguided way. I had a reputation, and I liked it.

My wake-up call came when, at the age of fifteen, I got arrested for a breach of the peace with anti-social behaviour and had to spend the night in a jail cell.

Not only was it a lonely and scary experience, but it landed me with a caution and a criminal record that would stay with me for the next five years.

I didn't realise it at the time, but looking back I feel quite fortunate that night happened the way it did, though I absolutely do not recommend or condone it in any way. That little cell, and the enormity of what it meant, finally got through to me in a way that my poor parents and teachers just couldn't, despite their monumental efforts.

Something clicked that night that, thankfully, stopped me in my tracks. I realised I had to be mindful of the company I keep and the influence others have on me. I knew I needed to make better choices. That I *could* make better choices.

It wasn't going to be easy. I'd been so used to backchatting and rebelling, I had a lot to learn (and unlearn). But the difference now was that I had motivation – a purpose – because under no circumstances did I *ever* want to end up back in that cell.

• • •

Not long after my night behind bars, I walked into a recruiting office in Blackpool town centre and signed up to join the army. I'll admit it wasn't my first choice of career, but despite my parents and teachers telling me to stop messing around and apply myself at school, my ignorance and bad attitude – not to mention my criminal record – now meant my options were going to be few and far between. Not many companies or colleges want to support someone who's been in police custody before their sixteenth birthday.

Fortunately, I was accepted as a frontline soldier in the Royal Armoured Corps. I was to be a trooper in the King's Royal Hussars, a main battle tank regiment, where I'd be sent to a place called Bovington in Dorset to learn how to drive a 62-tonne Challenger 2 main battle tank. I couldn't even drive a car yet!

● ● ●

Before I could go to Bovington, I had to head first to Winchester, a posh city in the south of England with fancy restaurants and locals who spoke like they still had their silver spoons stuck in their mouths. Aside from having some of the most expensive houses I'd ever seen, Winchester was also home to the Army Training Regiment (ATR), a place where I'd spend fourteen weeks doing my basic training.

When I arrived at Winchester Station, things didn't exactly get off to a good start. I was greeted by a sergeant who seemed to like the sound of his own voice, and before we'd even left the car park, he reprimanded me, first for being late and second for making a phone call to my mate. Me being me, I told him to chill out. It cost me my mobile phone for the next three days.

When I got to my dorm room, minus my phone, I sat on the end of my bed and took in my new digs. Twelve single beds lined the room, divided by metal lockers and a small chest of drawers. The eleven other lads arrived one by one, each mumbled a quiet 'hello' and unpacked their civilian clothes, kit and the few personal items that were allowed. I wondered what the next three-and-a-bit months had in store for us all.

It was then that I noticed there were words stuck on every wall. Words that, later, I would also see on posters in the cookhouse as I ate my dinner. Those words were:

COURAGE

RESPECT FOR OTHERS

INTEGRITY

LOYALTY

DISCIPLINE

SELFLESS COMMITMENT

To be honest, they didn't mean anything to me at first, but they were obviously important to someone. In the coming days and weeks, I'd learn that these words were the values of the British Army and the Army Cadet Force.

Words that, eventually, would come to be my values, too. Words that would help me navigate some of the toughest situations in my life.

VALUES

I've come to learn that what we're all living through at the time of writing is called a 'polycrisis'. It's where several disasters in a row (Covid, wars in the Ukraine and Gaza, a cost-of-living crisis, the effects of climate change etc.) shake things up so much that it impacts everyone. And guess what? Whether we realise it or not, that affects our mental well-being – our behaviour and the decisions we make.

And, polycrisis aside, our teenage years are often a wild and bumpy ride. You're not a kid anymore, but you're not exactly an adult either. Your body's changing, and you suddenly find yourself riding a rollercoaster of emotions you didn't even want to get on. School adds its own share of stress, of course. And let's talk about friends – they're awesome, but sometimes the need to fit in can make you say and do things you don't like.

As well as raising my own teenage daughter and doing what I can to understand a bit about her world, I'm lucky that I get to do a lot of work in schools and colleges, meeting amazing young people and talking to them about their plans for the future. In doing so, I've realised that a lot of you feel anxious about what's to come.

I can almost guarantee that during every school visit or conversation I have with a group of young people, as well as blowing me away with their curiosity, insight and open-mindedness, at least some of them will tell me that they:

- are uncertain about their future
- don't feel prepared for what's to come
- worry about their family's expectations
- are concerned about money
- doubt themselves
- feel pressure from friends and other peers

Some or all of those might sound familiar to you, too. And that's a lot on anyone's shoulders, isn't it?

I believe that at the bottom of all of these, what's fuelling these worries, is a feeling of lacking control. I know it was for me. And it's no wonder, when we're trained to always focus on the Next Big Thing – an exam, a job, a car, a pay cheque, whatever. For many, those things are overwhelming; for others, completely unachievable. But imagine if we could refocus. And instead of living life working towards someone *else's* expectations, we start to set our own paths. The exams or whatever else are no doubt there along the way, but they aren't everything.

How can values help?

Think of values as the stuff that makes you, well, you. Or at least, the version of you you'd *like* to be. They're the principles and beliefs that shape how you treat others, make decisions and live your life every day.

If being **kind** to others is a big deal to you, that's a value. Or if you think **honesty** is super important, that's another value. Values help you figure out what's right and wrong, what you stand for and what you want to achieve.

You've probably done those tests at school that tell you what kind of learner you are, hands-on or visual, or perhaps you've discovered whether you're more of an introvert or an extrovert. There's merit in knowing that about yourself. But those give an insight into who you already are – not necessarily who you want to *become*.

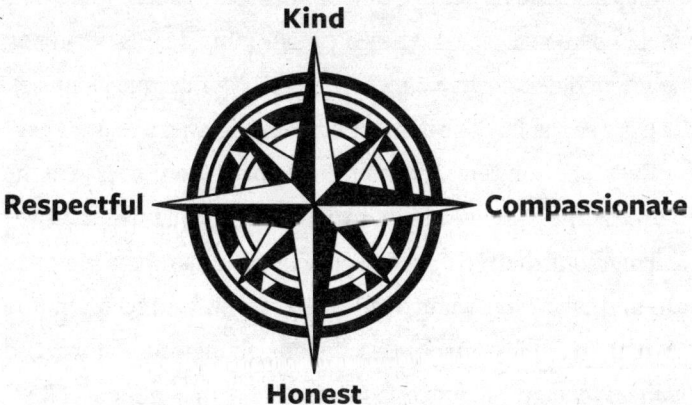

Kind

Respectful — Compassionate

Honest

Think of your values like a compass, pointing you in the right direction, guiding you towards a life that is happy, fulfilling and meaningful. Without them, or by following the wrong ones, you could feel unsure, anxious, adrift.

But I'd like to stress that living a life led by values doesn't mean you won't face tough times. You will – we all will – there's no way of avoiding it. What values can do is provide a roadmap to help guide you through.

The instructors I met during my training in Winchester lived and breathed their values, and they did their best to encourage new recruits to do the same from day one. But they could only really introduce us to them; it was up to us to do the rest. We had to choose whether we were going to actually *live* them.

Who decides your values?

Values have the power to guide our behaviour because they are deeply personal. They're based on our individual experiences, beliefs and perspectives, and they reflect our unique identities. They're shaped by our family, culture, religion and education.

Everyone's different, but I think your teenage years are the perfect time to start thinking about values (that was the age I learnt about them). You're beginning to understand who you are and what you want from life. It's also a time when you start to make life-changing decisions about your future, and values will help you make those choices with confidence. But I firmly believe that we're never too old, and it's never too late.

Values are one of the most important tools you'll ever own. You aren't born with them. No one else can choose them for you. You have to discover them for yourself.

How can values help us find our place in the world?

Values aren't just helpful when it comes to understanding ourselves, they can play an important role in our relationships, too. They provide a common ground for understanding and communication, helping us to connect with others on a deeper, more meaningful level. When we share values with others, it gives us a sense of belonging and community. In other words, they help you find your tribe.

Then again, when our values are at odds with others, it can lead to misunderstandings, disagreements, even conflict. A good way of knowing when to steer clear.

And it's not just about people, either. Making sure your values align with future employers will make you happier and give you more job satisfaction through your career. Buying from companies whose values match yours will make whatever you're buying all the better.

I'd love to see a future where our values are commonly shared in CVs or on social media platforms, just as we would a qualification, hobby, or anything else we're proud of. How cool would that be?

How often should we think about values?

Our values will always be with us, but they're not necessarily what we *think* about, more what we live by. They can be shaped by our experiences, so may change and evolve based on what happens to us. Often, they're the result of a whole lifetime of learning and growing. Mine have remained the same for nearly a quarter of a century, but I'm still learning about what each one means for me.

To begin with, you might have to write them down or remind yourself to think about them, but over time – and with practice – it won't be a conscious process. You'll learn to nurture and develop them without much thought at all.

What's the difference between goals and values?

I want to talk a bit about goals vs values, because it's easy to get the two confused.

Goals are specific objectives you set out to achieve in life. They're the targets you work towards in areas like school, work, fitness or relationships. But, especially when you're young, a lot of your goals aren't set by you. They're the steps you *have* to take to turn your dreams into reality. And they're usually something you want – or need – to accomplish within a certain timeframe, again not necessarily set by you. It's also likely your goals will change over time, as you grow and as your circumstances change.

Now, I'm not saying goals aren't helpful. They are – I have loads! I wouldn't have completed any of my extreme adventures if I hadn't set them as my goals. But it's important to remember they come and go. Values, on the other hand, are here, now and for ever. You can take ownership of your values at any age and apply them in any situation. You don't need a certain GCSE or amount of money in the bank.

It's also important to point out that it's possible to

achieve a goal but forget your values along the way. Let's look at an example:

Sam listed **self-acceptance** in her values. Separately, she set a goal to improve her physical fitness and decided she wanted to be fit enough to be able to comfortably run a 5km race. So, Sam pushed herself, trained hard and over time felt stronger. On race day, her dedication paid off and – incredibly – she managed to run the full 5km without stopping! But despite reaching her original goal, she felt like a failure. Sam couldn't stop wishing that her legs had got a bit leaner, her tummy a bit tighter. She compared herself with the other runners and felt her body didn't look as toned as theirs. In this scenario, Sam's goal was achieved but felt empty and meaningless because, whether she realised it or not, she'd forgotten about self-acceptance. She'd lost sight of her value.

When it comes to setting your goals, always ask yourself, 'How can I reach this goal while keeping my values intact?' It might take longer, it might be harder, you might even have to take a different journey to get there, but I promise you it'll be worth it.

How much of your life do you leave to chance?

I'm a firm believer that if you want to make positive changes in your life, you have to take things into your own hands. But that's not to say I don't believe in luck. I just believe there are two types.

The first is dumb luck, which is pure chance, perhaps finding a wad of cash tucked into the pocket of a second-hand coat.

Then there's constructed luck, the kind that comes from being practical and prepared yet staying open to chance. An example of this could be a person who has been consistently networking, improving their skills and staying open to new opportunities in their career. Eventually, they happen to find themselves in the right place at the right time to land a job offer that aligns perfectly with their aspirations. This success wasn't *just* a stroke of luck; it was a result of the proactive efforts that led them to that point.

Holding a set of values is a way of preparing us for, or opening us up to, opportunities. I guess you might call it manifesting. Either way, it requires us to think about our future and hold the belief that we can achieve great things firmly in our minds.

Life is full of unexpected twists and turns, after all.

Why wait?

There is no perfect version of you waiting in the future. You're here! Do what you can now to live life on your own terms.

Putting things off until tomorrow, next week or next year isn't going to help you. Now is as good a time as any. You'll be happier for it.

So, what are you waiting for?

CHOOSE YOUR VALUES

Now you know why you need values, it's time to start thinking about what *yours* might be.

Take a look at the list of values below, and if you can, see if you can choose between five and ten. Some of these values might represent characteristics you know you already have and want to develop; others, something you aspire to. If you think of something that's not on this list, that's fine, too. There are no right or wrong answers here.

A quick word of advice – don't overthink it! Trusting your gut is a powerful thing, and I'll talk more about it later in this book.

☐ Accepting	☐ Achiever
☐ Adventurer	☐ Adaptable
☐ Assertive	☐ Authentic
☐ Balanced	☐ Beautiful
☐ Bold	☐ Brave
☐ Brilliant	☐ Challenging
☐ Community-minded	☐ Compassionate

☐	Calm	☐	Capable
☐	Clever	☐	Competent
☐	Confident	☐	Consistent
☐	Courageous	☐	Creative
☐	Curious	☐	Determined
☐	Disciplined	☐	Decisive
☐	Dedicated	☐	Ethical
☐	Empowered	☐	Fair
☐	Friendly	☐	Fun
☐	Happy	☐	Honest
☐	Humourful	☐	Influential
☐	Inspiring	☐	Independent
☐	Individual	☐	Innovative
☐	Inquisitive	☐	Just
☐	Kind	☐	Knowledgeable
☐	Leader	☐	Learner
☐	Loyal	☐	Logical
☐	Open	☐	Optimistic
☐	Peaceful	☐	Positive
☐	Religious	☐	Reputable
☐	Resilient	☐	Respectful
☐	Responsible	☐	Securc
☐	Selfless	☐	Spiritual
☐	Stable	☐	Successful
☐	Trustworthy	☐	Wealthy
☐	Wise		

Don't worry if you're struggling to decide; self-reflection can be hard. If you want to, ask someone you know and trust what they'd pick from this list. You might find you've picked one of the same words as someone else but that it means something else to them, and that's fine! The whole point of values is what they mean to you, not anybody else.

You also might want to think about the values of the people you look up to. You respect them for a reason, even if you haven't really thought about what that is before. So, think about your role models – it could be someone you know or someone in the public eye – perhaps it's a sportsperson, musician or a YouTuber. Now ask yourself:

- What might their values be?
- How do you know?
- Why do those values inspire you?

Just as the army and cadets do, your favourite football club, sports team or clothing brand might share their values, too. Here's a few that might get you thinking:

Manchester United Foundation
- *UNITE*
- *NURTURE*
- *INVEST*
- *TOGETHER*

- EXCELLENCE
- DIVERSITY

NASA
- SAFETY
- INTEGRITY
- RESPECT
- INCLUSION
- TEAMWORK
- BALANCE
- INNOVATION
- EXCELLENCE

Nike
- COMMUNITY
- SUSTAINABILITY
- DIVERSITY
- SOCIAL RESPONSIBILITY
- DO THE RIGHT THING
- BE ON THE OFFENSE ALWAYS
- SERVE ATHLETES
- CREATE THE FUTURE OF SPORT
- WIN AS A TEAM

Greggs
- FRIENDLY

- INCLUSIVE
- HONEST
- RESPECTFUL
- HARDWORKING
- APPRECIATIVE

TikTok
- AIM FOR THE HIGHEST
- BE GROUNDED AND COURAGEOUS
- ALWAYS DAY ONE
- BE CANDID AND CLEAR
- BE OPEN AND HUMBLE

Don't see your favourite brand or organisation here? Loads of companies share their values on their website. Give it a google!

There's no reason you can't adopt the same values as someone or something you admire – it's exactly what I did all those years ago when I joined the army. But you need to understand exactly what those little words mean to you. You might feel as if you're not ready to choose all (or any) of yours yet, or you know the ones you like but can't explain why, and that's OK – you'll get there.

As you read through this book, look out for the **Check-point** at the end of every chapter. This is a chance for you to check in on your values and see what feels right for you.

If you've already chosen your values, that's great – well

done! But your next challenge will be to understand how you can live and breathe those values, not only in your day-to-day life but in the face of really difficult situations. Times when you're tested, challenged and pushed to your absolute limits are often when it's hardest to remember your values. But they're also when we need our values the most. In other words:

You've got to learn to walk the walk.

Even when the going gets tough.

Now, I'm going to show you how I live my life by *my* values, share times when I've been at my lowest, and demonstrate how those words – **COURAGE**, **RESPECT FOR OTHERS**, **INTEGRITY**, **LOYALTY**, **DISCIPLINE**, **SELFLESS COMMITMENT** – have pulled me through. And, you'll have to trust me on this one, they always do.

I hope it gives you some inspiration along the way.

COURAGE

WHAT IS COURAGE?

'Courage is not the absence of fear. Courage means you move forward in the face of fear.'
SHANA SCHUTTE

Have you ever felt nervous about doing something, but you went ahead and did it anyway? Well, that's courage.

Having courage isn't the opposite of feeling scared; it's feeling the fear and overcoming it. It's about not being rash or impulsive. It's about not giving in to peer pressure – choosing not to get into a mate's car when you think they may have had too much to drink but you're afraid of what they or others might say or think. Courage is assessing the situation rationally, analysing the risk and then doing what your gut tells you is the right thing.

Courage is needed in all kinds of situations, and there are two distinct types: moral courage and physical courage.

They're both equally important, but just as the cadets do, I see them as two separate things.

Moral courage

Sometimes, as in the example above, it's about resisting peer pressure. Having friends and doing things together is great, but if you know in your gut that what you're all doing – or about to do – is dangerous, unethical or just plain wrong, it takes courage to be the one to stand up and say no.

Other times, courage is needed to push you out of your comfort zone. It can be easy to get into a rut, doing the same things with the same people day in, day out. If you want your life to be more interesting, to see new places and do new things, you're going to have to grab opportunities when they come along. You're going to have to sign up for that trip, audition for a part in the school play, apply for a course, commit to raising money for a charity, train for a race, help plan an event. It's easier to say, 'Oh, I can't be bothered,' and settle back into your usual routine, but your life will be far richer if you push yourself to grab these opportunities and run with them. And that takes courage.

Sometimes you need courage to face up to family or relationship problems. It might mean standing up to family members; this takes real courage and you might need to get help from a trusted adult such as a teacher or other relative. Asking for help, by the way, isn't a sign of weakness; it's a sign of strength. It takes courage to end a relationship that feels wrong for whatever reason.

Physical courage

Physical courage is the ability to confront danger or discomfort. In the military, this means going into a conflict zone and facing the enemy. You're scared, nervous, apprehensive, but you do it anyway because it has to be done. It's the right thing to do. It's your job.

Perhaps, in some ways, it's easier to be courageous in the army than it is in civilian life. I know that sounds strange when we're talking about life-and-death situations, but there's a sense of duty, a stepping up together as a team or unit, that's less common outside of military life. The enemy is clear. You have a sense of purpose.

When I was stationed in Iraq, I lost my good friend LCpl Alan 'Bracks' Brackenbury to a roadside bomb while he was out on patrol. I'll never forget the dark day we lost Bracks. Our entire unit was devastated. But being in a war zone, where there's little time for grief, the next day a group of us had to get back out on the ground and along a route very close to where we'd lost our friend. We never spoke a word of it, but I know the others were all feeling like I was – scared like never before. But we knew we needed to show courage. It's what we'd all been trained to do. Personally, I never even questioned whether I was going to do it, because

I knew I would, and I did. And I know without a doubt that Bracks would have done the same.

Both moral and physical courage are important, especially for younger people like you. Moral courage will help you navigate ethical challenges in your life, whereas physical courage develops your ability to face adversity head on and build that all-important **resilience**. Combine them, and there'll be nothing you can't face.

It takes courage to be a soldier. Of course it does. But sometimes, it takes even more courage to confront the problems and issues that face us all in our everyday lives.

YOUR COMFORT ZONE IS YOUR ENEMY

Us humans are creatures of habit. We like to know things are stable and secure, and we're good at convincing ourselves not to do something. But your comfort zone is where you stagnate. You're not growing if you're in your comfort zone. So next time someone asks you if you want to do something you've never done before and you're not sure – provided it's relatively safe, within the law and aligns with your values – just say yes. You'll be amazed what you learn about yourself along the way, even if what you learn is that you don't actually like the thing you've just tried!

I try to push myself out of my comfort zone at least once every day. I've done some amazing things and met incredible people because of it, and I know with absolute certainty that I wouldn't have had those experiences if I'd stayed where I felt safe. In fact, I'd probably still be in the box bedroom back in my parents' house in Blackpool.

For you, this is particularly important. As a teenager, you need to experiment to know what you like and don't like. Trial and error is really the only way you'll understand it. And – I can't stress this enough – grab the opportunities when you're young. Things get much harder when you start to factor in jobs, responsibilities and relationships. There is no better time than now!

Everyday Adventure #1

This is a simple yet effective way to help you with your self-discovery. Use the notepad at the back of the book or open a note-taking app on your phone.

At the end of every day, spend five minutes reflecting on something that took you out of your comfort zone. It could be something small or more significant, anything goes.

Ask yourself:

- How nervous or anxious did you feel before doing it?
- How do you feel afterwards?
- Did you learn anything about yourself from the experience?

Gradually, as you become more comfortable with pushing

yourself, you can increase the challenge level. Before you know it, you'll be able to track your progress and see how far you've come, and how much confidence you've gained.

Struggling to get started? Here are some examples you could try:

- Strike up a conversation with someone you don't know well (even if it's just to say 'hello').
- Try a new food or recipe.
- Participate in a school club or extracurricular activity you've been curious about.
- Share your opinion in a group discussion.
- Take a different route when going for a walk or bike ride.

USE YOUR FEAR AS FUEL

Fear is a funny thing. It can help to keep you safe, but if it stops you from doing something that would benefit you or someone else, it's actually just keeping you small.

But – and I'm sure you don't need me to tell you this – pushing your fears to the back of your mind and pretending they're not there isn't going to do you any favours.

I used to think it was possible to overcome fears, that I *should* overcome them, but through age and experience I've realised that's not necessarily a helpful goal. Because by allowing yourself to *feel* the fear you can turn it around, harness it, use it to motivate you and push you forward. It's a healthy, rewarding process. And once you win those internal battles, the external ones become a lot easier.

If I'd listened to my fears, I would never have promised a little boy called Ibrahim that I'd build him a school

It was late 2018 and I was visiting Djibouti, a small country in Africa where a quarter of the population live in poverty. One day, I was invited to an orphanage in a village just outside of the capital.

One boy, Ibrahim, took an immediate shine to me, sticking to me like glue as I went around on my tour. I learnt he'd been through a lot in his short life, but despite everything, he was a happy little guy with a huge grin.

Through an interpreter, we had a long chat, and he told me about his dream to go to school. A school that, sadly, didn't exist in that part of Djibouti. One day, he said, he'd really like to be a teacher, so he could help other kids like him.

Our conversation stuck with me for a long time after.

I made a decision: I was going to build him, and all the other kids like him, that school. I'd need to jump through political hoops, convince a lot of important people, and – here's the kicker – somehow raise $350,000.

I was scared I would fail him, and scared of what it would take to build an entire school, from nothing, 4,000 miles away from home.

But I had to push through the fear of the huge promise I'd made to someone, and try my hardest to make it happen. That promise, and the fear that I couldn't do it, pushed me forwards and lit a fire in my belly to reach my goal. And guess what? I did.

I hope my story shows you that you can learn to embrace your fears, big or small, if you're willing to face them head on.

But I'm aware that's a difficult ask, and that for some people, the fear is so powerful it can be debilitating. If you feel like that, the next EVERYDAY ADVENTURE could help.

Everyday Adventure #2

There's a technique you can use to help face your fears called *gradual exposure*. It involves slowly but systematically confronting your fear or phobia in a controlled and safe manner.

There are a few methods you can use, my favourite is called The Fear Ladder, but it's critical that whatever you choose, you go at a pace that suits you. Be patient and take your time. Facing the things you fear is no small feat.

The Fear Ladder

Step 1: Write it all down

Make a list of things you're afraid of. For example, if you're afraid of social situations (social anxiety), the list may include saying 'hi' to a neighbour, asking a stranger a question, making small talk with a cashier, or making a phone call.

The Fear Ladder

You might have a lot of different fears. If so, it can help to group similar fears or specific fear themes together. Make different lists for different fear themes.

Step 2: Build your fear ladder

Once you've made your list(s), arrange the items from the least scary to the most. To help you do this, you can rank how much fear you have for each situation, ranging from 1 (very mild fear) to 10 (extreme fear). Once you've ranked each situation, fill in your Fear Ladder. Put the things with the lowest number at the bottom, working your way up to your highest number at the top.

Using our case of social anxiety from before, here's an example:

- Giving a presentation to a room full of people – **10**
- Talking to an authority figure, such as a supervisor or teacher – **9**
- Participating in a group discussion – **7**
- Going to a party or social event that may include people you don't know – **6**
- Making a phone call – **5**
- Ordering food at a restaurant – **3**
- Saying hello to a neighbour – **2**

If you have a lot of different fears, you can create separate ladders for each.

Step 3: Set your goal

Now you've made your Fear Ladder, it's time to identify a specific goal that you want to work towards. This might be whatever the top ranked fear on your ladder is, or it might be something a bit broader. For instance, and once again using our example, this could be giving a presentation to a room full of people, or maybe to be more confident in any social situation.

Step 4: Facing the fear

You're going to tackle the situation that causes the least anxiety from your Fear Ladder first. Using our example, this would be 'saying hello to a neighbour'. Now – and this is the part where you really do have to get out of your comfort zone – you need to start doing that activity repeatedly. Every day, if you can.

By doing it over and over, you'll soon start to feel less anxious doing it. If the situation is one that you can remain in for a prolonged period (such as going to a social event), stay long enough for your anxiety to lessen. This will be different for everybody, as only you know how you're feeling. And then, once you feel ready, you can work your way up your ladder – one step at a time.

The reason this works is that as you repeatedly face your fears without any harm coming to you, your brain starts to form new connections. It learns that the fear isn't as dangerous as it initially thought, changing your response to the situation.

The Fear Ladder

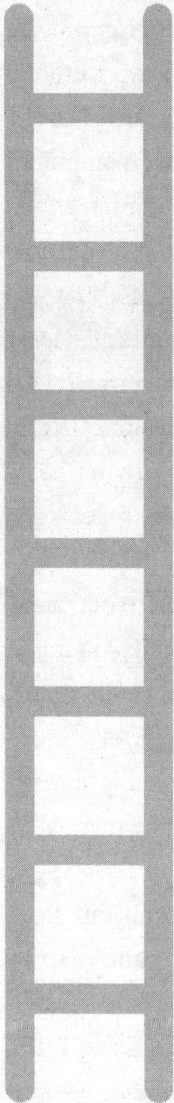

....

....

....

....

....

....

....

Step 5: Practise, practise, practise

The more often you practise, the faster the fear will fade. Some steps can be practised daily, while others can only be done once in a while. It's important to plan exposure exercises in advance, as that way you'll feel in control of the situation. Always identify what you're going to do and when you plan to do it.

And don't forget to maintain the gains that you've made. Even if you've become comfortable doing something, it's important to keep doing it so your fears don't creep back in.

Remember, you're not necessarily aiming for a 0 or even a 1, as experiencing some level of fear can be a healthy, helpful thing.

Step 6: Celebrate your victories

As you progress up your ladder, you might want to occasionally step back and re-rank your list. This will help you to see how far you've come and what an amazing job you're doing.

It's not easy facing your fears, so make sure you reward yourself when you do it. It's an incredible achievement! You could even plan a special reward or treat to mark your milestones.

On the other hand, don't be discouraged if your fears start creeping back in. This can happen from time to time, especially during stressful periods or big life events. This is normal. It just means that you need to start practising again. And hey, you've done it before, you can do it again.

Remember that facing fears is a process, and it's essential to be patient with yourself. Over time and with lots of practice, you'll build a confidence and resilience that'll last you a lifetime.*

ESCAPE THE ORDINARY

When we do the same things day in day out, life can feel a bit dull. Doing things that take you away from the everyday are great for your mind and your soul. I could never have imagined half of what I've done in my life, but by staying open to doing things that are out of the ordinary, I've had experiences that have left me inspired and fulfilled. I'm always looking for where my next adventure will take me – cycling from Pisa to Blackpool on a bike made from sustainable recycled materials, perhaps?

But I think courage is also to be found at home – finding happiness in the day-to-day. It's something I've struggled with all my life. I'm just not very good at sitting still!

Of course, there are things we can't avoid. Beds need to be made, dishes need to be washed, laundry needs to be folded. Respecting these things is important. But I have a little motto: make the mundane interesting. It's about using the headspace a boring task gives you to let your thoughts

---

* If the fear is particularly challenging or persistent, you might consider involving a professional who can help. Have a look at the list of resources available to you at the end of this book.

run wild. So, when I'm polishing my shoes (a habit that's stuck with me from my army days), I let my mind buzz with plans and ideas for the future. I use that time to plan ahead. To look forward.

Whether we like it or not, our bodies and brains need a break. We can't go at 100mph all the time or we'll burn out. So, learn to go slow. Take your time. Choose when to charge forward.

OWN YOUR MISTAKES

Everyone makes mistakes. I've made some huge ones that, at times, I didn't think I could get past.

Even while writing this book, I made another. A big one.

For a year or so everything had been going my way. I was riding high off the back of my MBE, my next adventure was beginning to take shape and I'd got engaged to the incredible lady I'd met in 2019. Life was as near to perfect as I could have imagined.

But I have a tendency to get caught up in things. And, without realising, I became hyper-focused on my work. I was saying 'yes' to everything. I was away all the time. Even when I was home, I wasn't really present. It wasn't about money; I'd learnt that lesson already. I guess it was just about feeding my ego. Selfishness in many ways, I suppose.

I totally neglected to think about the impact my choices were having on my fiancée. And one day, seemingly out of the blue, she left. Except it wasn't out of the blue. I'd subconsciously been ignoring all the warning signs for months. The future I'd imagined for us disappeared in an instant. I would have given anything to turn the clock back and do things differently. But that's not how life works, is it?

Over time, I've learnt that how we choose to move on from our mistakes is the bit that counts.

I need to tell you now that living a life led by values won't stop you making mistakes or getting things wrong. It's not going to shut out difficult situations. There'll be times when you fall in with the wrong crowd, do something stupid through peer pressure or lose control of your temper.

But your values will help you to feel safe in the knowledge that you are in the driver's seat of the decisions you make, the paths you choose and also how you respond to challenging situations. You are in control.

So, when you slip up – which you will, take it from me – you need to learn to acknowledge it and work out how you move on. My three-step process can help:

1. Admit it to yourself.
2. Talk it over with a trusted adult.
3. Go back to your values and ask yourself where things went wrong.

Remember, just one mistake, or even a few, isn't the end of the world. You won't be defined by it. It's how you move on that matters.

Tips
- Try to push yourself out of your comfort zone wherever possible
- Don't beat yourself up if you make a mistake – just be sure to learn from it
- Remember to be patient

Checkpoint

Now you've had a chance to think about **courage**, how do you feel about including it in your own values? If you like some of the themes but are not sure it's the right fit for you, you may be inspired by some similar values from the list below:

- **Bravery**: acting without hesitation in the face of fear or difficulty.
- **Boldness**: demonstrating confidence and a willingness to take risks.
- **Resilience**: bouncing back from setbacks and difficulties with strength.
- **Daringness**: embracing challenges and new experiences with a sense of adventure.
- **Tenacity**: holding onto goals despite obstacles and setbacks.

- **Adventurousness**: willingness to step into the unknown and explore new territories.
- **Steadfastness**: remaining committed to your principles and goals, even in tough times.
- **Endurance**: sustaining efforts and maintaining resolve over a prolonged period.
- **Persistence**: continuing efforts despite difficulties or repeated failures.

RESPECT FOR OTHERS

WHAT IS RESPECT?

'Good manners will open doors that the best education cannot.'
CLARENCE THOMAS

What do I mean by having respect for others?

In a nutshell, it's treating other people the way you'd like to be treated yourself. Would you like to be bullied, ignored, laughed at? Of course you wouldn't. You'd feel scared, upset, maybe even ashamed. And that's why you don't behave that way to others.

You may be thinking, well, that's not fair; I'm a nice person. I'd never bully anyone.

That's great, but having respect for others goes a lot further than that. Think about some of the adults you know. I bet some of them are teachers, right? When I was at school, I didn't think about my teachers as people at all. I was too busy being the class clown and getting a laugh at their expense.

Now, I feel ashamed of my behaviour. The teachers were trying to do their job – educating us – and I was making that job a whole lot harder. Never for one moment did I think about their feelings, how frustrating and upsetting it must have been to be in that situation.

Today, I have the utmost respect for education and for teachers everywhere.

How about old people? Do you even notice them, apart from getting annoyed if they're clogging up the pavement with their Zimmer frames and mobility aids? But every old person was a young person once – a young person just like you. If you take the time to talk to an older person about their experiences, you might find they're a bit more interesting – a bit more human, even – than you thought. And you might have a lot more respect for them.

But respect isn't just about other people. It's also about you. It's knowing that you're a worthwhile human being with needs, wants and rights that are deserving of respect. Knowing how to treat yourself with respect is just as important as treating other people with respect. In the rest of this chapter, we'll explore these ideas a bit further.

NAVIGATING THE ONLINE WORLD

As a lad, I didn't have access to the internet. No one I knew had ever heard the words 'social media', let alone considered a world dominated by it. Growing up is very different now. I know it is for my teenage daughter. And doing the job I do would be very hard without it.

But it's not going anywhere, so we've got to decide for ourselves how we let it into our lives. And, most importantly, how we apply our values and behaviours in a virtual space.

Everyday Adventure #3

My daughter and I came up with some guidelines to help keep her happy and safe online. If you can, I recommend you do the same, perhaps with a trusted adult.

When you've finished your list, consider saving it as your phone wallpaper or printing a copy to keep next to your computer. Keep it easy to hand and remind yourself to review it regularly.

Here's a few to get you started:

- **Think before you post**. Always be mindful of what you share online, whether it's photos, messages or videos. If you're not sure, don't post it.
- **Guard your personal information**. Your privacy is easily compromised. Avoid sharing personal details like your full name, address, phone number, bank details or school with strangers or on public platforms. Keep that information safe and only share it with trusted individuals.
- **Be careful on social media**. If you use social media, make sure to understand the privacy settings and adjust

them accordingly. Only accept friend requests or connections from people you know in real life. Remember, not everyone is who they claim to be online.

- **Be kind and respectful**. Treat others online the way you would in person. Choose your words carefully and communicate respectfully, even if someone else is being rude or disrespectful. Think before you respond and always aim to be kind.

- **Stand against cyberbullying**. Cyberbullying is never okay. If you witness someone being targeted online, speak up and offer support. Always report any incidents of cyberbullying to a trusted adult or the platform itself.

- **Be content critical**. The internet is filled with misleading information. Learn to question and verify the accuracy of what you read or see online. Use reliable sources and be aware of the presence of misinformation and fake news.

- **Find a balance**. Remember to balance your online activities with offline experiences. Engage in outdoor hobbies, spend time with friends and family, and enjoy other interests beyond the digital world. Life is about so much more than screens.

- **Seek guidance from adults**. I want you to know that you can always come to me or another trusted adult if you have any concerns or problems online. We are here to help and support you through any challenges you may face.

- **Be inclusive**. Embrace the diversity of our world and treat others with kindness and respect. Celebrate different

perspectives, cultures and backgrounds. Make an effort
to include and uplift others online.

- **Trust your instincts**. If something feels off or uncomfortable online, listen to your instincts. Remove yourself
from any situation that doesn't feel right and seek support when you need it.

The time I had to disconnect to reconnect

Some people might refer to me as an 'influencer'. It's not
something I would ever call myself, but with over 100,000
followers on all my social platforms and that little blue tick
next to my name, apparently that's what I am. I've no doubt
my social status helped me in my career – I've used it to
raise funds and bring awareness to charitable causes and
opportunities. But with it I've also gained trolls, abuse, negative thoughts and jealousy.

This all came to a head at the end of the Great British
Paddle, my attempt to circumnavigate the UK by paddle-
board, when I returned home to a world full of Covid restrictions, uncertainty and not a lot else. I retreated further
and further into my phone, addicted to the dopamine hits I
was getting from the stream of likes, swipes and comments.
Thankfully, by this point in my life I was self-aware enough
to know when I was falling and knew exactly what I needed
to do. I went to my failsafe – my values – and decided I
needed to make a change.

So, on World Mental Health Day 2021, I announced I was

going to delete all my social media accounts. Not just for a day or two, but for a whole year.

It was a bold decision, one that raised a lot of eyebrows. It wasn't an easy choice, considering how much of my life – professional and private – revolved around digital platforms. But it was time to break the chain. And so I said farewell to the constant notifications, comparisons and mindless doomscrolling.

The year that followed surprised me in ways I could never have imagined. Here's what happened:

I rediscovered connections
Without superficial interactions keeping me busy on social media, I found myself investing time in my real-world relationships. I made new friends and got to know old ones better. I grew closer with my daughter. Turns out it's much easier to have a good chat with someone if you've not got one eye constantly on your phone.

I embraced solitude
I'd never been very good at being on my own. But, in the absence of constant notifications, I discovered the power of silence and the ability to listen to my own thoughts. This headspace allowed me to properly reflect on my goals and values. It's where I dreamt up my next big adventure!

I appreciated the present moment
Without the constant urge to document every outing, event

and experience in the name of content, I learnt to live in the present moment. Whether it was an amazing view, a good conversation, or a meal out, I appreciated each experience for what it was. Nothing more, nothing less.

I learnt to be true to myself
Social media sometimes encourages us to present a public version of ourselves – the one we want everyone else to see – and along with that comes a pressure to look or behave in a certain way. During my year off, I rediscovered the joy of just being Jordan. Not the one on the cover of my books, on TV or presenting a TED Talk, but the one who isn't afraid to admit he doesn't always have the answers. The one who enjoys a kickabout in old joggers.

I revived old hobbies
I'm sure I don't need to tell you that social media is an absolute time sucker. Imagine putting all that time and energy you spend staring at your phone into a hobby! Well, that's exactly what I did. With my newfound time and focus, I jumped straight into planning my next challenge, got back into playing football and tried new things. I did things just for the joy of it, and what a feeling that was.

I woke up to fake news
Social media can be a double-edged sword when it comes to sharing news and information. It's great for fast news – I'm

willing to bet most global events of the past ten years have broken via social media before they make it anywhere near a news channel or a newspaper. It's where I learnt of the death of our late Queen. But during my year off, I learnt to be much more mindful of where I get my news from. Without hashtags and Twitter trends, I was forced to find other sources, from multiple places, and realised that your choice of news outlet can affect your thinking. Stepping away from that echo chamber allowed me freedom to form my own thoughts and opinions.

I reconnected with nature

I don't want to sound like some kind of tree hugger, but when I freed myself from digital distractions, I remembered how good it feels to be immersed in nature. There's a name for it: green therapy. Spending time in the outdoors walking, wild swimming or just sitting in the sunlight gave me an enormous sense of gratitude for our world and a kick up the backside to do more for our environment.

I don't think it's an exaggeration to say that my year off social media gave me a totally new view on life and the world. Above all, it was a game-changing lesson in respect – respecting those around me, respecting myself and respecting the natural world.

My advice to you? Take a break! Not necessarily for a year, but perhaps a morning, a weekend or a holiday. Find the balance. Build better habits. Ration your use. Do it out of respect for yourself and those around you.

MANNERS MATTER

There's a posh boys' school near where I live now whose slogan is 'Manners Maketh Man', or put simply, manners make the man (or woman). It's a school that's many worlds away from my old comprehensive, but I have a lot of respect for their motto.

In a world where communication is routinely reduced to instant messages and emojis, manners may seem a bit old-fashioned. You might even think they're completely re-dundant. But I believe good manners are a cornerstone to a happy life, both personal and professional. Especially so as a teenager, when showing good manners can make a huge difference to how you're seen by others.

And it's simple stuff, isn't it? Saying please and thank you, respecting other people's time by not being late for school or work. In the army, we used to say, 'If you're on time, you're already late,' which meant we were always where we needed to be at least five minutes before.

But for some reason this straightforward set of rules that are – let's face it – pretty easy to follow are often forgotten. I know I've been guilty of it myself.

My teenage rebellion

I mentioned before that I put some of my bad behaviour as a kid down to a lack of control. I felt like I wasn't in charge of my life, and I knew I wasn't cut out to be the person everyone else seemed to want me to be. I felt the need to do things that I suppose, in a misguided way, gave me some sort of identity.

So, I was rude. I challenged authority. I guess, like many teenagers, I questioned the rules and norms imposed on me. Rebelling against teachers seemed like a way to assert my independence. It was my way of breaking free from what I saw as restrictions and control.

And I craved the attention of my classmates. I wanted to be the cool kid, the funny one, the joker.

Disruptive behaviour also gave me an escape from the mundane aspects of school life. An injection of excitement into an otherwise predictable routine and daily environment.

Of course, it was short-sighted. While it temporarily provided a little thrill, it came at the cost of my education, personal development and relationships with teachers and other students.

As I've got older, I've learnt to recognise the importance of **self-respect**, **respect for others**, **responsibility** and **genuine connections** over that fleeting feeling of coolness. That's not to say I don't still challenge people – I do   I've just learnt to approach it very differently.

Who'd have thought that the bad-mannered lad would one day be honoured by His Majesty the King at Buckingham Palace? Certainly not me.

Everyday Adventure #4

Let's explore exactly how and where manners can make a difference to you, not just in your day-to-day life but when it comes to achieving your goals and getting what you really want out of life.

I've included a list of scenarios you're likely to face below. As you read through them, put a tick next to the response that feels most like something you would do:

1. A friend is telling you all about their weekend in way too much boring detail.

   Do you:

a. Make yourself listen, then when they've finished, ask a further question or make a comment about their weekend. ☐
b. Half-listen, while working out in your mind a story about your own weekend you're going to tell them as soon as you can get a word in edgeways. ☐
c. Glaze over, and when another friend walks past you, go and join them, leaving your original friend mid-sentence. ☐

2. It's the end of your weekly football training session. Before rushing off to a hot shower, do you:

a. Stop briefly to thank the coach and tell him how this training session has helped you. ☐
b. Shout a quick 'thanks' to the coach. ☐

c. Get off the pitch as quickly as possible so you'll be first in the showers. ☐

3. You're waiting to be called in for an interview, feeling a bit nervous. When you're finally called in to the room, do you:

a. Say hello, smile at everyone in the room and wait to be instructed on when and where to sit. ☐
b. Put on a bit of swagger to hide your nerves, grin broadly at your interviewers and say, 'Hi, how you doing?' ☐
c. Try not to catch anyone's eye, mutter a quick hello and sit down on the only available chair. ☐

4. You've arranged to meet a friend you don't see very often. On the day, though, you're pretty tired and don't feel like going. Do you:

a. Perk yourself up and go anyway, even though you don't feel great. ☐
b. Message them to say you can't make it. ☐
c. Go back to bed and sleep for two hours. When you wake up it's an hour after you were due to meet, so there's no point in messaging now, is there? ☐

5. Somebody's giving a presentation at work or college. Do you:

a. Put your phone on silent and leave it in your bag. ☐
b. Leave it on the table so you can easily see it if you get a message. ☐
c. Sit at the back and play 'Minecraft' on your phone (on silent) to keep you entertained during the boring bits of the presentation. ☐

6. Every single year your great-aunt sends you the lamest birthday present ever: a £5 Amazon gift card. Do you:

a. Send her a message the next day thanking her and mentioning what you are planning to spend it on (even though you might have to save up a bit more first). ☐
b. Send a brief 'thanks for my gift card' message, but only because your mum has nagged you about it for nearly three weeks. ☐
c. Not bother. £5 a year? What a joke. ☐

Now, go back through your scores and jot down which letter you ticked the most.

If you ticked mostly As, great work! You're conducting yourself as well as you possibly can. But remember, manners can be lost in an instant, so try to always keep them in check.

If you ticked mostly Bs, good job. You're showing some decent manners, but there's perhaps still some room for improvement.

If you ticked mostly Cs, you haven't yet mastered your manners. You need to do a bit of work to improve them if you want people to respect you. I've explained a bit more about how this can help you below. You can do this!

Good manners aren't just about making other people feel good. Here are some of the ways your good manners can help *you*:

Build positive relationships

Like it or not, a lot of what we count as 'success' in life depends on making people like us, or at least take us seriously. Which is definitely not to say that we should be 'people-pleasers', intent on pleasing others at the expense of our own well-being. Building positive relationships isn't about trying to be what you're not, but there are things you can do to make other people view you in a positive light. Things like listening, respecting other people's point of view even if you don't fully agree with it and trying to put yourself in the other person's shoes. Smiling helps, too!

Enhance communication skills

By using polite language (no swearing or rudeness), actively listening to the other person, maintaining eye contact and thinking about body language (open and friendly, rather than defensive or aggressive), you can open communication channels and encourage other people to listen to what you're saying.

Display respect

Good manners are all about respect. Respect for other people's feelings, point of view, beliefs and boundaries. Putting yourself in the other person's shoes. Remember what we were saying about treating other people in exactly the same way you'd like to be treated yourself? That.

Nurture friendships

Politeness and good manners are like oil for an engine. In social situations – that is, any situation where you are interacting with other people – they help everything work much more smoothly. Not only that, but by being considerate and supportive of other people, and by showing gratitude where appropriate – everyone appreciates a 'thank you' – you can establish stronger connections and lasting friendships.

Boost self-confidence and create a positive self-image

Fun fact: when you behave well towards other people, you feel better about yourself. Knowing you've treated other people just like you'd want to be treated yourself gives you an inner rosy glow. Not only that, it helps with confidence and self-respect. It's a win–win!

Prepare you for life

Wherever you're heading, be it to college, uni, training or the world of work, good manners can give you an edge.

Good social skills, of which good manners are a huge part, help convince employers and others that they want you on their team. This can lead to all kinds of useful things, such as internships, mentorships and future collaborations.

HONESTY IS THE ONLY POLICY

Hands up, I've told lies in the past. Who hasn't? I'm sure you can think of a few.

Studies show that teenagers are the age group most likely to tell fibs. It might be about getting out of trouble, a way of protecting someone else's feelings or a middle finger to authority. Whatever it is, you lie because you crave the ability to make your own decisions and choices, which is a natural process at an age and stage when you're focused on forging your own identity.

But dishonesty has an awful habit of coming back to bite us. I know this all too well.

A lie that got out of hand

After an exhilarating overseas expedition to Sierra Leone six years ago, I arrived home eager to share my adventures with friends, family and my (albeit relatively modest back then) social media following. But there was a problem – a big one. When it came to uploading the photographs I'd taken with my slightly battered digital camera, I realised that my photos were, quite frankly, rubbish. Totally unusable.

A shot of panic surged through me. What was I going to do? I told myself that if I shared those pictures, I'd be a complete laughing stock. I had absolutely nothing to show for my hard work. What an amateur.

But then a thought crept in. I ignored it at first, as I knew it was wrong. But I couldn't get it out of my head. Before I knew what was happening, I'd opened Google and was frantically typing words into the search bar:

> 🔍 Professional photographs of xxx

And, of course – the wonders of the internet – up popped a selection of beautiful pictures taken by a photographer I'd never heard of. Shot after shot of the very same views I'd so clumsily tried to capture myself.

You won't be surprised to hear what happened next. I scooped all the photos up into a folder and saved them as 'Jordan's Photos' on my desktop. Next, I uploaded them one by one to my social accounts, all credited to Jordan Wylie.

I watched the likes, comments and DMs roll in.

This looks incredible!

Wow Jordan, amazing photos.

Great work.

Problem solved. Or so I thought.

Little did I know, one of the photos I'd posted had been widely used in the media recently. In the unforgiving world of social media, it didn't take long until I got caught out. I quickly deleted the posts, but it was too late. Word spread and, inevitably, it reached the ears of the photographer whose photos I'd so hastily stolen.

I felt sick when I saw his name pop up in my inbox. His message was a complex mix of emotions – disappointment, anger, hurt. He shared his journey with me, explaining what it had taken to capture those photographs. The toil, the dedication, the countless hours devoted to realising his ambition, the sacrifice. It was a story I knew well – it could have been my own.

I felt an overwhelming sense of guilt. Not only had I disrespected the photographer, but I'd compromised my values in the process.

I offered a heartfelt apology to him, acknowledging the pain I'd caused. But I knew the words alone weren't enough. I needed to rebuild what had been broken – I needed to live by my value of **respect for others**. For me, this meant publicly confessing what had happened, crediting the photographs to their rightful owner and actively promoting his work whenever and wherever I could.

The repercussions of my dishonesty went way beyond that single act of theft. After the immediate embarrassment and stress passed, I forced myself to confront the inner demons that had led to my poor decision-making. And, believe me, any temporary gains I'd won by the lie were far outweighed by the damage I caused to both myself and those around me.

This story is often at the forefront of my mind, even all these years later. I know now that true growth and fulfilment can only be achieved in living life with total honesty. Even if you think it's protecting someone else, or that it won't hurt anyone, there are very few instances where a lie will make things better. As with most things, the simplest path may not be the best one.

Tips
- Treat others the way you'd like to be treated yourself
- Don't try to get away with things you know you shouldn't be doing
- Respect is as easy as having good manners

Checkpoint

There's a lot to think about when it comes to **respect for others**. Was there anything that surprised you? It's now time to have another think about your own values and whether you want to make any changes. You might be inspired by some of these similar values, too.

- **Courtesy**: treating others with politeness and consideration.
- **Kindness**: showing compassion and empathy towards others.
- **Tolerance**: accepting and valuing differences in opinions, beliefs and backgrounds.
- **Open-mindedness**: being receptive to different perspectives and ideas.
- **Empathy**: understanding and sharing the feelings of others.
- **Equality**: treating everyone with fairness and impartiality.
- **Appreciation**: recognising and acknowledging the value of people and things.
- **Consideration**: thinking about the impact of your actions on others.
- **Diversity**: embracing a range of backgrounds, cultures and perspectives.
- **Inclusivity**: ensuring that everyone feels welcome and valued.
- **Ethics**: conducting yourself in a morally upright and responsible manner.

INTEGRITY

WHAT IS INTEGRITY?

*'Real integrity is doing the right thing, knowing that
nobody's going to know whether you did it or not.'*
OPRAH WINFREY

As a child, I spent my summer holidays at football
camps, hanging around with boys I didn't know from
other schools. Being a group of football-obsessed kids
from the north-west of England, the first thing we'd always
ask each other was, 'What team do you support?' Despite
being a lifelong Blackpool Football Club fan, I would always
answer 'Manchester United' without hesitation. Why? Because that's what everyone else said, and I was desperate to
fit in. Blackpool FC weren't anywhere near as good as Man
U, and I was worried I'd be laughed at.

I'm sure I wasn't alone in telling these untruths. Whether it's a band, brand of school bag or even a career choice

– people will do and say all sorts to feel accepted and be part of the crowd. So much so that sometimes the person we are and the person we *pretend* to be can feel completely different.

But the more we do this, the more we become imposters in our own lives. Eventually, your authentic self gets lost behind a make-believe version of you. This is why we need integrity.

Having integrity is about accepting that you don't need permission from other people to be yourself. It's about being true to yourself and your values and not being swayed by others' opinions. Ever.

That's all easier said than done though, isn't it?

CHOOSE YOUR OWN PATH

You are unique. There is only one of you, and your life is yours to live as you choose. Sounds straightforward, doesn't it? But think how often you're swayed by peer pressure, by family pressure, by social media pressure, by wanting to fit in, by wanting to please others, by being afraid of how others will react. Living your life on your own terms is a lot harder than it first appears.

The trick is to cultivate your own internal sense of who you are and where you want to be. Again, this is quite hard. It's easier just to go with the flow, to go along with others' expectations, to think that what 'everyone' wants, whether that's lots of money, a flash car, glamorous holidays or a particular appearance, is what you want too.

Well, it might be. But you're not a clone of them – you're you. Unique. Different. Full of potential. So choose your own metrics of success. Decide what *you* want out of *your* life. And if you don't really know what you want, you're going to have to try out as many different situations and experiences as you can until you've found something that you really love. Something that makes your heart sing, that makes you go '*Yes!!!* This is it!'

Okay, perhaps it sounds a bit cheesy, but the point is that you shouldn't be comparing yourself to others, and their – seemingly – perfect lives. In reality, no one's life is perfect, and you can't expect yours to be. But if you've carved your own path, followed your own values and stayed true to them, it will be the best life it can be.

The only competition you need to worry about is yourself

Following my own path has been an incredible journey of self-discovery. It's given me a sense of freedom and empowerment. I've learnt to trust my intuition and make decisions that align with my values and goals. It's led to experiences that I wouldn't have had if I'd simply followed the crowd.

One of the biggest lessons I've learnt is the power of embracing my uniqueness. Accepting who I am – the good, the bad and the ugly – and building genuine self-confidence.

In 2013, I fell into what turned out to be my first proper expedition

It wasn't the result of a lifelong dream, and I sure-as-sh*t hadn't made any long-winded strategic plans. It was all very simple.

Ryan, a mate of mine in the military, very sadly lost a close family member to cancer. He knew almost instantly he wanted to do two things: he wanted to raise some money for a cancer charity, and he wanted to climb a mountain. Mount Kilimanjaro, to be exact.

Dubbed the Roof of Africa, Kilimanjaro is the highest peak on the African continent and the biggest freestanding mountain in the world (it's not part of a mountain range like Everest in the Himalayas).

Ryan came to me and our other mate Callum with his plan. I had no hesitation in accepting the challenge, but I couldn't help my thoughts running away with ideas about how to do it differently. Thousands of people climb Kilimanjaro every year, from all around the world. It's a great challenge and a tough climb, but we had to do something to stand out and bring awareness to the cause.

So, I suggested we climb it barefoot.

Of course, both lads thought I was off my rocker. But I doubled down. I suggested we climb it barefoot and call the project 'Barefoot Warrior'. They still weren't convinced, so we agreed they would do it their way, I would do it mine. All good.

I set about organising a website, a logo... Looking back, I guess I was building a bit of a brand.

Anyway, we climbed it. Ryan and Callum with their shoes firmly on, me without so much as a stitch from my knees down. My mates raised £1,000 for the charity, a lot of money by anyone's standards and a good job done. But by thinking outside the box, doing it in a way that surprised and frankly baffled most people, I was able to drum up enough support to raise over £70,000.

Of course, my feet were absolutely filthy, and I came away with a few superficial cuts, grazes and some rock-hard skin. Nothing that a good scrub and a pedicure wouldn't sort – the only time I've ever had one in my life! But looking down at my tattered trotters I realised just how adaptable the human body – my body – is. I've no doubt that doing it barefoot gave me a deeper connection with the adventure, its cause and the landscape itself.

Ultimately, we all climbed that mountain together. The only thing that I did differently was take my shoes off! But it showed me that you don't have to go with the flow. You can follow your own path and maybe, just maybe, achieve even bigger and better things than those who tread the well-worn one.

I've applied this mindset to all my subsequent expeditions. When I'm planning an adventure, I'm not looking to do what other people have done or to do it better. I'm looking at the things that are meaningful to me, the things I care about or want to make a difference to. And sometimes, that make things a bit harder, because there's no rule book. But I've learnt so much more about myself by doing things the way I want to do them. I've no doubt it's made me happier in the long run, too.

Don't get me wrong, there have been plenty of challenges along the way. There were, and often still are, moments of doubt and uncertainty, especially when I'm questioned or criticised for my choices. But these moments teach me **resilience** and the importance of staying true to myself, even in the toughest of moments.

Anyway, this is all to say that no one else is going to live your life, so don't spend it following in anyone else's footsteps. It isn't always easy, but any of us can do it if we keep working at it, and you'll find that it transforms your life.

AVOID SUMMIT FEVER

I talked a bit about the difference between goals and values earlier, but I'd like us to look at goals again, this time with integrity in mind.

When we think about our goals, it's important that we don't get so caught up in them that we miss out on other things along the way. Focussing all your time and effort on achieving something can come at the cost of your friends, family and other things that are important to you.

The process of getting to your goal is where the real

learning and success is – so try to stay grounded and appreciate all the parts of the journey that make it unique. Your goals will become meaningless if there's no one to celebrate with at the end! And that doesn't mean you shouldn't work really hard to reach your goals, but approach them mindfully and with an appreciation of all the parts – not just the end. There's no rush.

I learnt this the hard way

When I was in my early thirties, my army career behind me, I became managing director at an international maritime security company. Smart London offices, swanky business dinners and no-expense-spared trips to far-flung locations around the world. For the first time ever, I could afford the finer things in life, and I thought, 'This is it.' I even bought a new Porsche, a Rolex watch and a racehorse! I had it made, or so I told myself.

But as my career – and my salary – skyrocketed, my home life took a nosedive. My obsession with my job meant I was no longer present for my partner or our young daughter, Evie. Over days, weeks and months, things fell apart. Nothing could fix it.

I went to a very dark place after that. One that I only got through with a lot of help from my support network, especially my mum and my GP.

When the darkness lifted, I realised that somehow, somewhere along the way and without even noticing, I'd completely lost touch with my values. In my obsession to make something of myself, I'd lost sight of what really mattered. I didn't recognise the person I'd become.

But I knew I could get back to the old Jordan, because despite losing nearly everything I cared about, I still had my values. I just had to remember how to use them and apply them to my life every day.

ACCEPT FAILURE

Success doesn't come without failure.

For every mountain climbed, ocean sailed or depth explored, there will be countless failed attempts we don't hear about. Frustrating – yes – but we need to learn to accept these so-called failures as just another part of the journey.

When I set out on the Great British Paddle, my record-breaking attempt to circumnavigate mainland Great Britain on a stand-up paddle board, it didn't really occur to me that I wouldn't make it to the finish line.

But the year was 2020, and a fresh wave of Covid regulations put an abrupt end to it all.

After 150 days on the board, having negotiated jellyfish stings, the bad-tempered Irish Sea and the wild tides of Scotland, I had to come to terms with the fact that this particular mission was going to fail. There was absolutely nothing I could do about it. And it hurt – a lot – much more than any jellyfish.

The outcome wasn't what I wanted, but the experience brought me so much that I could never have predicted, particularly memories of kindness from total strangers.

I also discovered that failure and setbacks aren't the end of the world. In fact, they're valuable learning opportunities. Accepting failure taught me to view mistakes as stepping stones to growth, and to approach challenges with a more open mindset.

I've also come to realise that my interests and passions aren't fixed; they can evolve over time. Having to take different paths allowed me to explore aspects of myself I hadn't realised and discover new passions I didn't know existed. It's been a reminder that life is full of surprises and that personal growth is an ongoing process.

Everyday Adventure #5

Learning to accept failure is a tricky thing. If you need some help figuring it out, I recommend giving the next exercise a go. You'll need to enlist the help of a dependable friend or relative to help you with this one.

Failure Reflection
Choose your activity
Select an activity or task you'd like to accomplish. It could be something like a puzzle, a craft project or a sports challenge. Or it could be some homework you've been set – kill two birds with one stone and all that.

Set your goal
Decide for yourself what you'd like to achieve from the activity. Remember, the goal isn't necessarily to smash the task out of the park, but to learn from it.

Go for it
Give it a go! Bring your A-game and give it your best effort.

Reflect
Afterwards, go to your chosen friend or relative and have a chat about the experience. Ask yourself:

1. How did you feel when you encountered difficulties or made mistakes?
2. What did you learn from those challenges?
3. What could you do differently next time?

Find the wins
Whatever the outcome of your task, try and think about all the things that happened *because* of your experience, or the things that went well. If you had a deadline, perhaps you completed your task on time or ahead of schedule. Maybe you met someone new because of it.

Try again
If it didn't go to plan, that's OK. Sometimes you just have to draw a line, accept it and move on. When you're ready,

you'll be able to try the activity again, keeping in mind the lessons you've learnt.

Over time, you'll develop a more positive attitude towards setbacks and become more **resilient** in challenging situations.

I think Thomas Edison, the bloke who invented the light bulb, said it best:

'I didn't fail 1,000 times. The light bulb was an invention with 1,000 steps.'

Trust your gut

You know that little voice inside your head that guides you, even when you can't explain why? That's your gut instinct.

But it isn't actually anything to do with your gut at all. It's your brain gathering evidence to alert you to something. It might not be conscious, fully formed thoughts. It might be difficult to explain. It's like your brain is saying, 'Hey, I have a sense that something might be right or wrong here, but I can't point out all the reasons why.'

Your gut instinct can help you make decisions without overthinking. For example, if you're walking down a road and suddenly feel like you should cross to the other side, it might be because your brain picked up on some subtle signs of danger that you didn't consciously notice.

Gut instinct is based on your experiences, emotions and what your brain has learnt over time. Sometimes, however, it might be influenced by fears or biases. So, while it's great to listen to your gut feelings, it's also a good idea to ask for advice from people you trust when making big decisions.

The day my gut instinct saved my life

In 2021, I set out to run ten marathons across the ten coldest places on the planet. During one of the marathons in Alaska, I was running with a friend when I felt a strong sense that something was off. My friend, who was older and arguably more experienced, reassured me that everything would be fine, but I still couldn't ignore the overwhelming feeling in my gut. Suddenly – and without warning – the weather took a turn for the worse, and we found ourselves caught up in a violent blizzard, barely able to see our hands in front of our faces.

We had to decide – push on or turn back. It was a white-out situation either way. But despite being less than halfway into the marathon, I decided to trust my instincts and make the difficult decision to turn us back towards base.

As it turns out, my intuition most likely saved my and my friend's lives that day.

After returning to base, we learnt that an avalanche had fallen in the area we'd been running towards. Had I ignored my instincts and continued with the original plan, things could have turned out very differently for us.

Here are a few everyday examples of when you might consider trusting your gut instinct:

Personal safety

It's dark. It's raining. You've got off the bus, and now you've got a choice of routes to walk home. There's the longer way round, along a main road, or there's the short cut along a badly lit footpath. You just want to get home and out of the wet, but it's worth taking a few moments to listen to your gut. You just might be better off taking the longer, well-lit route after all.

Decision-making

You're faced with a choice of options. It could be fairly trivial, like what to have for lunch, or more important, like what course to choose at college. But if a particular option feels 'right' before you've had a chance to fully analyse why, it might be worth considering.

Relationships

Your gut has got a big role to play here. If something doesn't feel quite right in a relationship, listen carefully to what it's telling you. If friends are urging you to do something you don't really want to, or a new boyfriend/girlfriend is lavishing you with attention in a way that makes you feel a bit uncomfortable – or maybe they aren't giving you much attention at all – listen to your gut instincts. If something *feels* a bit off in a relationship, then it probably is.

Creative projects

Here's another area where following your gut can pay dividends. Whether it's making music, art, dance or problem-solving, try 'going with the flow' instead of overthinking everything. Your 'gut' might lead you to unique and interesting solutions that your conscious mind hadn't considered.

Job interviews

Remember, job interviews are a two-way street. If there's something about the atmosphere, the people or the kind of questions you're being asked that makes you uncomfortable, take note. It's probably not the kind of place you want to work in.

Listening to yourself

Over the years, I've had plenty of people telling me that what I'm planning to do is too difficult or just plain impossible. Whether it's rowing through pirate-infested waters, running across the world's most dangerous countries or raising more than a quarter of a million pounds to build a school, I was always told the same thing. If I'd listened to them instead of trusting my instincts, I'd have not achieved any of them. So bear in mind what other people are saying but listen to your gut as well. If it's telling you that you can do it, then go for it!

Tips

- Don't become constrained by other people's opinions
- Follow your interests as they change over time
- Trust your gut!

Checkpoint

Integrity can be a difficult concept to get your head around, but once you've cracked it, it can be a genuinely life-changing value to live by. Spend some time now reflecting on the lessons we've covered in this chapter and how they sit with you. Here are some other values you may want to consider, too.

- **Honesty**: truthfulness and transparency in all interactions.
- **Authenticity**: being genuine and true to yourself, not pretending to be something you're not.
- **Accountability**: taking responsibility for your actions and decisions, good or bad.
- **Trustworthiness**: demonstrating reliability and being worthy of trust.
- **Consistency**: Acting in a way that aligns with your values across different situations.
- **Responsibility**: fulfilling obligations and duties in a reliable and conscientious manner.

- **Reliability**: being dependable and consistent in your actions and commitments.
- **Transparency**: openness and clarity in communication, especially when dealing with others.
- **Fairness**: treating others fairly and impartially.

LOYALTY

WHAT IS LOYALTY?

'When people show loyalty to you, you take care of those who are with you. It's how it goes with everything. If you have a small circle of friends, and one of those friends doesn't stay loyal to you, they don't stay your friend for very long.'

JOHN CENA

When you think of loyalty, you might have visions of soldiers standing shoulder to shoulder in the line of fire. Together, willing to brave danger and sacrifice all for the sake of a greater good. Loyal to King, country and comrades.

And loyalty can be heroic, I've seen it in spades out on the front line. But it can also be small, quiet and compassionate.

One summer, when I was a young soldier, I'd been looking forward to taking my long-awaited two weeks' leave. I'd made plans for a little holiday and had been dreaming of a lie-in for months. At the same time, the guy I shared a room with, Smithy, was due to go on guard duty, a kind of military assignment, that would take him away for most of the summer. Tragically, and without warning, his mother died the day we were due to leave. Immediately and without hesitation, I offered to take over his duties so he could go home and grieve with the rest of his family. I did it out of loyalty not just to my friend but his family and, I suppose, the army.

It's no surprise that the army and cadets include loyalty in their values – in life-and-death situations, you need to know who you can trust.

But outside of these extreme circumstances, in the normal world, loyalty might look a little different. Your loyalty is a precious commodity, and you need to be careful you don't give it away too freely. To do that, you need to understand how to keep your wits about you, be smart and build genuine trust.

You might be thinking that loyalty is all about other people. But actually, we've got to start by looking a bit closer to home. Because sometimes, it's the loyalty we show ourselves that's most powerful.

BE YOUR BIGGEST ALLY

Believing in yourself and building the best version of 'you' is the greatest thing you can do for those around you. Just as commercial flight attendants will tell you during a pre-flight safety briefing, you must always deploy your own oxygen mask before you can help others.

Of course, that doesn't mean tearing others down along the way. You have to do it from a place of mutual respect and compassion. It also doesn't mean ignoring the mistakes you have made, and will continue to make, along the way.

It all starts with the conversations we have with ourselves

You know, the ones no one else hears.

How often is that voice – your voice – saying something positive? Stuff like, 'I'm really proud of the way I handled that situation today.' And how often is it saying something negative, thoughts like, 'Why am I such an idiot?'

It's bad enough when that type of negativity comes from another person, but it's even worse when it's coming from your own thoughts.

If I said the half of the stuff I've said to myself to other people, I'd have been beaten black and blue! So why is it acceptable to talk to ourselves like that? Well, to put it bluntly, it's not. So, we need to address it head on.

There's a name for this inner dialogue – self-talk. And the content of your self-talk matters because *you* are the most influential voice inside your head.

The next activity is designed to help you become more aware of your self-talk, understand whether it's negative or positive and learn how to shift your thinking towards a more positive outlook.

Everyday Adventure #6

I'd like you to think now about the way you talk to yourself in moments of quiet. Spend a day with the notepad at the back of this book or your notes app close to hand. Over the course of the day, jot down all the thoughts that enter your head, without filtering anything. After you've written it all down, put the notes aside for a bit. This break gives your mind a chance to shift focus, so when you come back to it, you'll see your thoughts with fresh eyes. As you read it back, pay attention to any patterns. Do you often find yourself worrying? Are you overly critical of yourself, no matter the situation? Do you sometimes feel like you can't achieve your goals? What kind of messages do you tell yourself? What labels do you use? What advice do you give yourself? Try to answer these questions and determine whether your self-talk is helpful or hurtful. If you discover negative self-talk, keep reading to learn how to make it more positive.

Swap out negative thoughts

Imagine you're a person who gets anxious when having to present in class. You think you're not good enough and that your teacher and classmates can tell you're nervous. This is an example of negative self-talk, and I'm sorry to say it doesn't do you any favours.

But what if you could change your negative thoughts to positive ones? When you're aware of your self-talk, you have the power to replace negativity with positivity, which in turn can improve your mood, behaviour and decision-making.

Now let's say you're working on a project and you make a mistake. Instead of beating yourself up about it, your inner self-talk tells you that mistakes are normal and just another part of the learning process. You reflect, continue and move on.

Encourage yourself

As shown in the example above, taking control of your self-talk will help you when you're challenged or face difficult tasks. You can coach yourself through any situation, reminding yourself of what you already know or what comforts you. One way to do this is by imagining how a kind and supportive friend or family member would encourage you. Think about what they would say and adopt that attitude when you talk to yourself.

Choose better labels

Pay attention to the labels you use for yourself. Negative words like 'loser', 'stupid' or 'lazy' can become self-fulfilling prophecies. Challenge yourself to use healthier, more accurate labels that guide you towards your goals.

You might catch yourself saying some of the following things:

- 'I'm a failure.'
- 'I'm stupid.'
- 'I'm lazy.'

If you do, try rephrasing it. You could say:

- 'I can improve how I tackled [a particular task].'
- 'I have the opportunity to learn about [a particular subject].'
- 'I'm not feeling motivated [right now].'

Everyone makes mistakes. Learning from them is what counts.

Be your own friend

If your self-talk tends to be negative, try treating yourself as you would a friend. Imagine projecting your self-talk onto an imaginary friend and hearing their feelings. You'd likely respond with empathy and kindness. Now, replace the friend with yourself and speak to yourself with the same compassion. The negative self-talk might not disappear immediately, but you'll drown it out with a stronger, kinder voice.

Find truth in negativities

Rather than accepting negative self-talk as truth, see it as a distorted message with some useful information hidden within. Probe your negative thoughts for kernels of truth and nuggets of wisdom. The harshest self-talk often contains a grain of truth. So, distinguish what's true from what's distorted. This way, you can extract some valuable insights from your self-talk.

Rescue yourself

You don't need someone else to rescue you – you can do it yourself. In stressful moments with negative self-talk, recognise that it's harming you. Make a conscious choice to shift to positive self-talk. This empowers you to identify your feelings, process them, seek help if necessary, find solutions, and take action.* You can guide yourself through tough times.

Reanalyse information

Reassurance is reminding yourself of what you already know, while reanalysis is reflecting on new information to discover something new. Don't shy away from new information or feedback, even if it's a bit scary. If you base your self-talk in fear, you can prevent yourself from benefiting from it. Embrace new information as an opportunity for growth and self-improvement.

Of course, there are other methods out there that might suit you better. Some people snap an elastic band around their wrist every time those negative thoughts creep back in. Those moments of brief physical pain eventually rewire the brain to say 'no'. But it's important to remember with any of these activities and techniques that nothing good comes easy. It takes time and patience to reprogramme.

Once you've become your own biggest ally, you can focus on the rest of your team.

---

* You can check out the list of resources available to you at the end of this book.

ASSEMBLE YOUR COMRADES

Do you sometimes feel you're the only person in the world feeling the way you do? That nobody understands or could help you, even if they wanted to? That you're basically alone?

John Donne, who was a poet way back in the early 1600s, wrote that 'no man is an island, entire of itself'. What he meant was that all human beings are connected to each other and that this human connection is absolutely necessary for every person to survive and thrive.

In the army and the cadets, you're always part of a tight-knit team. You work together to achieve a set goal, and you always have each other's back. But out in the real world, you can sometimes feel that no one cares about how you feel or what happens to you – or if they do care, they're too busy or distracted to help.

The key point here is that you're *not* alone. There are people who are, or could be, on your team – you just need to work out who they are. Friends and close family members are obvious candidates, but what if your friends are busy with their own problems, and you don't think your close family would or could understand?

Then it's important to assemble a wider team. First, you need a trusted adult. This could be a member of your wider family – say a grandparent, an aunt or an uncle. Maybe a teacher at your school – one you like and find it easy to talk to – or a youth club leader. A medical professional such as a doctor or the school nurse. A social worker, the school counsellor, a school librarian, the team coach – someone you feel you can trust. Make a list of these people – there will probably be more of them than you thought!

Secondly, people of your own age. Apart from friends (and we're not talking about being Mr or Miss Super-Popular here; two good friends are more valuable than twenty flaky ones), who else could be a member of your squad? Brothers and sisters, cousins, members of your sports team, choir or drama group? Make a list of those who you think you could share some news with, or ask a question of, or ask for help. People who seem kind, empathetic and open. Again, there will probably be more of them than you first thought, and even if that's not the case, it's quality not quantity that counts.

Hopefully, looking at these lists will reassure you that there are people out there you could speak to if you needed to, who would listen and be able to help. So even if you're not a soldier or a member of the cadets, you are not an island, and you're definitely not alone.

Sometimes, all you really need is just one person

One person who *gets* you. One person who you can share your thoughts and fears with safely, with trust and without judgement. One person who won't give up on you, who has your back through thick and thin. Someone to just be there when you need them the most. Someone who says, 'I've got you,' without actually saying anything at all.

As you get older, you really do realise that quality is far greater than quantity. If you're lucky enough to have one of these people in your life, hold onto them with everything you've got.

And maybe you can be, or already are, this person for someone else.

As I mentioned earlier, loyalty should always be a conscious choice, based on understanding and critical thinking. It should be about acknowledging both strengths and weaknesses, pros and cons, before choosing to stand by someone or something.

There will be times in your life when staying loyal to your values might win over staying loyal to a particular person. Loyalty should always bring other values into play, too, things like honesty and integrity.

But the reality is that there will be times in your life when your loyalty is pushed to its limits.

The time my loyalty backfired

I'd always been loyal to a childhood friend. We shared a lot of memories and had supported each other through various ups and downs. One day, when we were in our twenties, he asked me for a loan to help him start a new business. I could see he was passionate about his idea, and he promised me that he'd repay the loan within three months.

I had a few reservations about handing over the cash – we weren't talking about a small amount of money – but he was my mate and I believed in him. So, choosing to ignore those niggling feelings of doubt, I decided to give him the loan.

After a while, I started to notice some red flags. The business didn't seem to be moving forward, my messages were being ignored and there was no sign of any money. I was getting a bit concerned, but I didn't want to confront him in case it ruined our friendship. It would all come good eventually, I told myself.

It didn't. That promised three months turned into years, by which point my own financial situation had changed. I needed that money, but instead of explaining my position to my mate, I held back. I was resentful, frustrated, and our friendship hit breaking point.

Eventually, I had to make the decision to let the money go and move on. For me, the effect it was having on my mental health was worse than the financial hit.

In this scenario, it'd be easy to put all the blame on my mate for what he did. But looking back, I've realised I have to take some of the responsibility, too. Here's what I could have done differently:

- **Improve communication**. I could've tried harder to talk to my friend about the situation and given him the opportunity to explain his circumstances in an open and honest way. There were probably things we were both unaware of.
- **Set boundaries**. It would've been a good idea for us to

set clear terms and expectations from the beginning, things like discussing a repayment plan with timelines.

- **Be realistic**. Three months was probably not a realistic deadline for my friend to repay the loan. We needed to work together to come up with a repayment plan that was more manageable.

- **Consider the impact**. I know now that I didn't properly consider the effect the situation could have on our friendship. I could have asked myself, 'Are you willing to risk this friendship?' By ignoring that difficult question, I didn't consider every scenario.

- **Protect myself**. I could have sought legal advice or an agreement from the beginning that would have helped me recover my money. Or, instead of giving away my own money, I could have helped my friend look into an alternative loan provider, like a reputable bank.

As important as these lessons are, the best thing you can do for yourself is understand how you can be loyal in a way that means you don't ever end up in a situation like mine.

How to avoid people taking advantage of your loyalty

Avoiding people taking advantage of your loyalty involves a combination of self-awareness, setting healthy boundaries and effective communication. Here are some steps you can take:

- **Self-awareness**. Understand your own values, needs, and limits. Be clear about what you are willing to give and what you expect in return. Knowing your own boundaries will help you recognise when someone is trying to exploit your loyalty.
- **Assess relationships**. Evaluate the people in your life. Pay attention to their actions, not just their words. If someone consistently takes without giving back or only reaches out when they need something, it might be a sign that your loyalty is being taken advantage of.
- **Healthy boundaries**. Set clear boundaries for yourself. Communicate these boundaries to others and be consistent in upholding them. This can prevent people from crossing the line and taking advantage of your willingness to help them.
- **Say 'no'**. It's important to learn to say 'no' when someone asks for something that goes beyond your capabilities or comfort level. Saying no doesn't make you a bad person – it's a way to protect yourself and ensure that your loyalty isn't misused.
- **Communication**. Be open and honest about your feelings. If you suspect someone is taking advantage of your loyalty, communicate your concerns calmly and assertively.

Remember, healthy relationships are built on mutual respect, give and take, and genuine care for each other's well-being. It's important to surround yourself with people who value you for who you are and not just for what you can do for them. Every situation is unique, and it's important to approach each one with empathy, understanding and a willingness to find a solution that works for both parties and respects the boundaries of the friendship.

Tips
- Don't expect your loyalty to never be tested
- Remember that there is always support out there for you
- Be mindful of the things you say to yourself – would you say them to others?

Checkpoint

How do you feel about including **loyalty** in your values? As we've covered in this chapter, it's a value that you have to tread carefully with, but once you get it right, the benefits are huge.

Here are some other values you could consider that share a lot of the same principles as loyalty:

- **Commitment**: being dedicated and invested in fulfilling your responsibilities.
- **Trustworthiness**: building trust by being reliable and keeping your promises.

- **Allegiance**: pledging loyalty and support to a person, group or ideal.
- **Dedication**: devoting time, effort and resources to a particular cause or relationship.
- **Dependability**: being reliable and consistent in the fulfilment of your obligations.
- **Consistency**: maintaining a steady and unwavering stance in your commitments.
- **Honourableness**: upholding a sense of duty and integrity in your actions and decisions.
- **Steadfastness**: resolutely staying loyal and unwavering, regardless of challenges.

DISCIPLINE

WHAT IS DISCIPLINE?

*'I've learnt over the years that freedom
is just the other side of discipline.'*
JAKE GYLLENHAAL

All the previous values I've talked about are worthwhile, but none of them will mean much without discipline, or to be more accurate, self-discipline.

So, what is self-discipline?

It's the difference between achieving your goals and spending the rest of your life thinking, 'I wish I'd...'

It's going out for a run even when it's raining and cold.

It's knuckling down to that homework or revision session when you'd rather be relaxing with your mates.

It's sticking with that course, job or activity that you don't much enjoy but that will help you get to where you really want to be.

It's deciding not to eat that pizza or burger and opting for something healthier instead.

It's sorting out your environment – your room, your study area, your belongings – and keeping it sorted.

It's going to bed early enough that you're not too tired to get up in the morning.

It's sticking with something you find difficult, whether it's school, work, a sport or learning something new.

Sounds a bit of a pain, right? A bit boring? But I'm here to tell you that self-discipline is one of the most important skills you will ever learn. Without it, you'll never achieve your goals. Yes, it's not fun turning down a night out with your mates because you've got an exam the next day. It doesn't feel great heading out to exercise when it's wet and cold and you'd rather be playing a video game or getting another hour in bed.

But discipline is the key to achieving anything worthwhile in life.

In the army, discipline is at the core of everything we do. It's so you can execute orders quickly and intelligently under the most difficult conditions. Insistence on performing tasks properly – whether it's how you wear your uniform or your marching technique – means repeating them until you can perform instinctively.

Without discipline, you could never build a cohesive team you could rely on.

And it's just as important in civilian life.

But here's the good news: there are ways to make self-discipline easier. In the following pages, I'm going to reveal some lessons I've learnt over the years that'll help. Think of discipline like a muscle that can be developed and strengthened over time – little by little, things like looking after yourself, staying organised and putting the work in get easier, so you need less willpower to achieve them.

HACK YOUR HABITS

Why is it that when we think of habits, we think of bad ones? Picking your nose, biting your nails, chewing with your mouth open – all the stuff you're told not to do. But habits don't have to be bad! In fact, if you can turn something into a habit, incorporating it into your life in a way that means you hardly notice you're doing it, it'll make that thing much easier to do.

And there are lots of other reasons we might we want to harness our habits:

- **Efficiency and automation**. They help you do everyday tasks easily, so you have more brainpower for fun stuff.
- **Consistency**. They keep you on track, so you can reach your goals and build good things over time.
- **Behavioural change**. You can use habits to make positive changes, like getting healthier or learning cool stuff.
- **Time management**. Habits save you time by making

decisions automatic. No more wasting energy on trivial choices.

- **Goal achievement**. Consistently engaging in activities that align with our goals increases the likelihood of success.
- **Mindfulness and awareness**. Some habits help you stay in the moment and know yourself better.
- **Overcoming procrastination**. Habits kick procrastination in the backside. You just do things without delay.
- **Mental and emotional well-being**. Certain habits, like exercise, boost your mood and make you feel great.
- **Personal growth**. Habits help you grow by giving you the time and headspace to learn new stuff.
- **Coping mechanisms**. They're a constant during tough times, giving you a sense of stability and control.
- **Social connection**. Some habits, like keeping in touch with friends, will help you build and keep awesome relationships.
- **Character development**. Good habits shape your character and make you a better person to be around.

Of course, everyone's habits will be different, but the discipline – that muscle we talked about earlier – is the same. It's about making time to do the things that matter and overcoming the reasons *not* to do something.

Here are five life-changing habits that I've worked hard over the years to incorporate into my daily life:

1. **Exercise**. My choice of exercise depends on my mood and whether I'm in training for an expedition, but essentially, it's about doing something – anything – that gets my heart rate up. It's good for my body and good for my mind.

2. **Cold exposure**. Every morning I spend thirty seconds or more under cold water at the end of my shower. This trains my brain and body to cope with stress and boosts mood. One of the quickest but also the hardest of my habits!

3. **Getting out of my comfort zone**. As we've already discovered in the chapter about **courage**, regularly challenging ourselves to get out of our comfort zone is important. When I reflect on what I've achieved at the end of the day, it's another opportunity to celebrate the wins – big or small.

4. **Screen-free time**. Having an hour a day where I don't look at my phone (or any other screens) is something I've done regularly since my year off social media. It gives me time to focus and knuckle down on my to-do list, as well as giving my eyes a blue-light break.

5. **Eight hours of sleep**. Sleep is something I used to think could be easily sacrificed. If I was busy, I'd stretch my day and go to bed late. Surely an hour here or there won't make any difference? But getting your body and mind into a rhythm of rest is important, even more so for teenagers because you're in a time of very fast physical, intellectual and emotional growth.

Can you think of any positive habits you have or would like to make? They might be about being more organised – making your bed or putting your clothes away. Or maybe they're about taking care of your mind and body – drinking more water, making healthier meals or building a walk or YouTube tutorial into your day. Reminding yourself of your values is also a very good habit to get into.

The saying goes that you have to do something sixty times to turn it into a habit. That might sound like a lot, and I'm not saying it's easy. But if you start doing it today, right now even, you could be doing that thing – whatever it is – almost automatically in just two months' time. That's roughly the equivalent of half a term at school.

Don't forget the advice on pages 33–4 about ways you can use the headspace that habits free up to think ahead and plan something exciting!

Habits are great for the day-to-day. But there will be times when you need to dig deep to achieve a goal or stay true to one of your values.

ALWAYS GET OUT OF YOUR SLEEPING BAG

When I'm in the thick of an expedition, I find the hardest part of the day – my biggest mental hurdle – is just getting out of bed. It's hard to find the motivation to get up and get going when the weather's bashing my tent, my kit and clothes stink to high heaven and every inch of my body aches. Staying wrapped up in my sleeping bag, where it's warm and toasty, always seems like the better option.

So in those moments of doubt, I force myself to think of the end goal – the reason I got myself into whatever bizarre situation I'm in – and work backwards from there. Because everything becomes easier when you've got a clear goal and a step-by-step plan to get you there.

Next time you think you can't do something, sit down and make a plan to do that thing – no matter how impossible it might seem – because most of the time that's all you need to show yourself that you can. You'll surprise yourself if you give it a go. And it's doing the hard things when you think you can't that builds your character and shows you what you're made of.

CONTROL THE CONTROLLABLES

Things don't always go to plan. In fact, they often don't. You can spend months or even years preparing for something, obsessing over every possibility, but it's inevitable that things will crop up and surprise you. Sometimes, the universe just has other plans.

This theory was confirmed to me when, on only the fifth day of the Great British Paddle, we lost our support boat, the *Coyote*. One of the most important elements of the whole expedition, the *Coyote* was to be my and my support team's accommodation, the place we'd make and eat our meals, our mission control, and our home (albeit a very cold and damp one). But a fuel leak rendered the thing not just useless but actually dangerous, and she had to go. It was a cruel setback for sure, but not for a second did I consider packing in the whole paddle. So, rather than shrugging our shoulders and turning our backs on months of hard work and tens of thousands of pounds of donations for charity, the team and I rallied. We came up with a Plan B (and C and D, just to be on the safe side). It wasn't perfect by any means, but the paddle continued.

As you know, ultimately the expedition wasn't meant to be. But we turned what could have been just five days into 150 days at sea – along with over £100,000 donated to charity – and I consider that a huge success. That came down to controlling what we could and accepting what we couldn't.

DON'T SWEAT THE SMALL STUFF

When I was in the army, small details were really important. Everything had to be polished and preened as if our lives depended on it (which, to be fair, they sometimes did). But looking back, I think it was mostly about showing **respect for each other** and that sense of **belonging**, being part of the team. Fair enough.

As I've gained more life experience, I've realised that the

small stuff isn't half as important as I once thought. When I'm up on a mountain or running a marathon in the Antarctic, those small details that used to consume so much of my mind just don't seem so significant. Don't get me wrong, my kit needs to be in good order and my nutrition and hydration taken care of – some corners just can't be cut. But for me, obsessing over the small stuff was leading me to set impossible standards that I couldn't possibly maintain, and it was sucking the joy out of every experience.

I now know that perfection doesn't exist; my best is good enough. But it can be hard to know where the line is – what's worth spending the time and effort to get absolutely right, and what's not – and it will be different for everybody. Your values can help you with these sorts of decisions.

The real breakthrough comes when you can work out what's imposed discipline, stuff that you feel is important to other people, vs self-discipline, stuff that's important to *you*. Remember that not everything can have the same level of importance, so prioritisation is key.

Everyday Adventure #7
Priority Pyramid

This is a great activity to help you work out what's important and what isn't.

To start, I'd like you to write down all the tasks and activities that make up your day-to-day life. This could include things like school assignments, clubs, social events, hobbies or chores. If it helps, write down the days of the week and what you typically do on each of the days.

Next, you're going to place each of the things on your list into the pyramid below, using the following criteria:

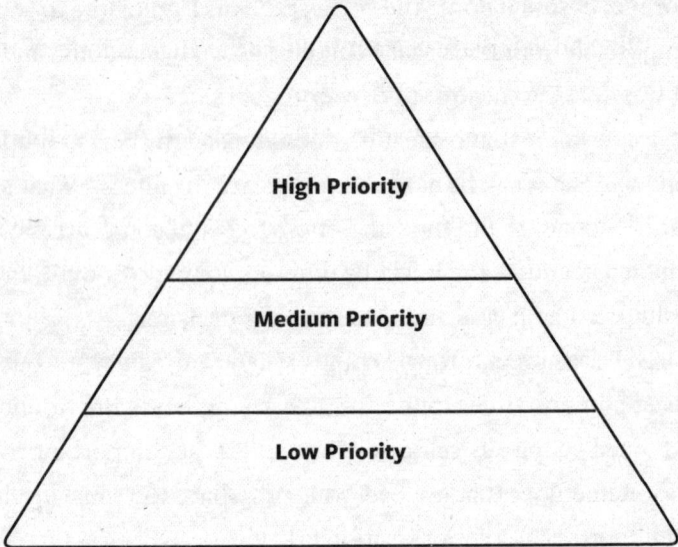

High Priority
This section will contain the tasks and activities that have the most significant impact on your values and goals.

Medium Priority
This section will include things that are important but may not have an immediate or critical impact.

Low Priority

This section will be made up of the stuff that's less important or could be considered a time-filler.

I'd like you to think about the potential outcomes and impacts each task has on your short-term and long-term goals. Now, ask yourself:

Why did you place certain tasks in the High Priority section? What makes them important?

How did you decide which tasks to place in the Medium Priority section?

What criteria did you use to categorise tasks as Low Priority?

Spend some time reflecting on your pyramid and consider whether you need to make any adjustments. Are there tasks that could be moved to a different section? Are there any tasks you initially thought were important but realised might not be?

Now, focus on the tasks from only the High Priority section. These tasks will be your priorities for the upcoming week. For each one, create a simple action plan with a few specific steps you need to take to accomplish it and set a reminder to check in with yourself at the end of the week.

At your check-in, ask yourself how you felt. Did you notice any positive changes in your productivity or stress levels? Do you feel like you could comfortably take on a bit more? Or do you feel happier when you don't have so much on your plate?

There will be weeks and maybe even months when you're able to do everything on your list, even the low priority tasks from your pyramid. But if you're ever feeling anxious, overwhelmed or even just a bit off, try sticking to only items from the High Priority list for a bit. You'll feel safe in the knowledge you're moving in the right direction, but you won't be adding any unnecessary stress or worry.

Tips
- Build good habits by doing things little and often
- Picture the end goal to get yourself through the hardest moments
- Making yourself do something difficult now will allow you to do something amazing in the future

Checkpoint

Now that you've taken some time to reflect on **discipline**, do you think it has a place in your values? Below are some related values that might resonate with you.

- **Control**: managing impulses and emotions to stay focused on goals.
- **Dedication**: being fully committed and focused on tasks and objectives.

- **Perseverance**: continuing efforts despite challenges and setbacks.
- **Responsibility**: fulfilling obligations and duties.
- **Commitment**: demonstrating dedication and loyalty to your responsibilities.
- **Resilience**: bouncing back from difficulties.
- **Patience**: enduring delays and challenges with a calm and composed attitude.
- **Consistency**: maintaining regular and steady efforts over time.
- **Precision**: paying attention to details and accuracy in tasks.
- **Accountability**: taking ownership of your actions and their outcomes.
- **Structure**: establishing routines and systems to guide actions and decisions.

SELFLESS COMMITMENT

WHAT IS SELFLESS COMMITMENT?

'Wherever you turn, you can find someone who needs you.
Even if it is a little thing, do something for which there
is no pay but the privilege of doing it. Remember,
you don't live in a world all of your own.'
ALBERT SCHWEITZER

One of the greatest lessons I've learnt in life? It's not all about me.

Don't get me wrong, receiving that letter from Buckingham Palace to tell me I'd been awarded an MBE, having my name on the *Sunday Times* Bestseller List and seeing my mug on primetime telly all felt pretty damn good. But I can honestly say that it's not what keeps me going through the twenty-sixth mile of a marathon in temperatures of -30°C or pulls me out from under my duvet on my darkest days.

Out of all my values, **selfless commitment** – putting the needs of others before my own – is the one that really sets a fire in my belly. It's the one that, for me, makes the most difference between doing something and not doing something.

It's that fierce determination to help, even when it's tough

In my lifetime, I've raised over £1 million for charity. That's a phenomenal amount of money by anyone's standards and no doubt sounds very impressive. But it's not what makes me tick. It's what that money – or just a tiny fraction of it – means to someone, somewhere, and how it's changed their life for the better. The human element. Stories like little Ibrahim's and all the children in his village who are now getting up in the morning with a purpose: to go to school. I genuinely think I could get to £1 billion and my attitude would still be exactly the same.

If you can make a difference to improve other peoples' lives, then you absolutely should – no matter who you are. All of us – every single one – can make a difference in this world, however small it may seem.

It's not about grand gestures. You don't need to conquer peaks to change lives – a simple act of kindness can make a mountain of difference. Whether it's standing up for what's right or supporting a friend in need, your actions matter more than you know.

Even in the chaos of conflict zones, where it seems as if people have nothing to give, I've come across people who've demonstrated remarkable selflessness.

When I was Afghanistan in 2018 running my first ever marathon, I rocked up for a few weeks without much thought about my living quarters. I needn't have worried. The locals blew me away with their kindness. They didn't have much but offered what little they did, sharing their food, their shelter and their hope. I'll never forget it.

Selfless commitment is a universal principle that can be practised every day. It's the friend who lends a listening ear, the neighbour who helps with the wheelie bins, or the stranger who donates blood. It's the force that binds communities.

Think about *your* community – your school, your friends, your family. There's always a chance to make a difference somewhere, and we all have our role to play.

Let's have a closer look at the reasons why you might want to include **selfless commitment** in your own values:

1. **Putting others first**. Being willing to prioritise other people's needs and happiness over your own doesn't mean you neglect yourself, but it's about showing kindness and empathy to others.

2. **Helping without expecting reward**. When you help someone or do something good for them, you do it because it's the right thing to do, not because you want something

in return. This could be helping a friend with homework without expecting them to do the same for you.

3. **Developing empathy and compassion**. Understanding how others feel and trying to make them feel better when they're going through a tough time. For example, comforting a friend who is upset, even if you don't benefit directly from it.

4. **Giving back**. Selfless commitment might involve volunteering your time or resources to make a positive impact in your community. It's about doing good deeds without expecting payment or recognition.

5. **Small acts of kindness**. Small gestures, such as holding the door for someone, complimenting a classmate, or helping a family member without being asked can go a long way.

6. **Playing the long game**. While selfless commitment may not always bring immediate rewards, it will lead to stronger relationships, a sense of fulfilment, and a reputation for being a trustworthy and caring person. Good karma and all that.

7. **Leading by example**. You can be a role model to others by sharing stories about your experiences and how helping others has made you feel good.

8. **Setting Boundaries**. While selflessness is important, it shouldn't come at the expense of your own well-being. You can't always say yes to everything and everyone, and it's okay to say no when necessary.

You're never too young to make a difference, so go out there and be the change. This world could use a little more kindness.

THE NEED TO LEAD

Do you think of yourself as a leader?

You might already be a natural – taking control in group exercises or being a captain for your sports team.

On the other hand, you might think it's something that you're not at all interested in – that you're happy to let someone else take the reins.

You might have no idea either way.

In life, and particularly through your career, there might be times when you *need* to step up. In the world of work, as you climb the ladder and take on more responsibilities, you'll likely reach a stage where you're expected to manage one or more people – whether you want to or not!

The cadets teach us that **selfless commitment** is critical when it comes to good leadership. That it's all about putting the needs of others ahead of our own to serve a greater good.

I have to admit, I'd have never thought of myself as leadership material. And although I may not have taken on traditional leadership roles, being an ambassador for the cadets, speaking in schools, becoming a father and even writing this book have all tested my leadership skills in one way or another. Most of what I've learnt hasn't been because of expensive training programmes or sitting in a classroom, it's been through making a tonne of mistakes. But, crucially, I've had to be hard-headed enough to admit where things have gone wrong and learn from it.

Leading doesn't have to be about fancy job titles, putting yourself out there or telling people what to do. Have you heard of the term 'leading by example'? If you simply live by your values – whether it's being kind, showing determination or practising good manners – you'll influence those around you to do the same.

STAY IN THE GAME

This is the 'commitment' part of selfless commitment. In the army, selfless commitment might mean making the ultimate sacrifice and laying down your life for your mission, your team and your country.

Obviously, that's at the extreme end of what selfless commitment involves. In everyday life, it's more about not giving up when the going gets tough. Even if you don't reach the goal you set out to achieve, just staying in the game can put you on the path you were meant to tread.

I've been lucky enough to have been on the receiving end of other people's selfless commitment at various points throughout my life. Through thick and thin, my parents have always stuck by me. Despite my wobbly start (and many other wobbles since), they never once gave up on me.

Similarly, through the highs and (many) lows of the Great British Paddle, my team were always with me, urging me on when I didn't know I had it in me.

That's commitment.

PAY IT FORWARD

Paying it forward is the idea that you repay kindness done to you by going on to do something good for someone else. This creates a chain of goodwill that will help many, many more people than the person doing the original act of kindness could have imagined.

In order to pay it forward, you first have to remind yourself of all the good things in your own life and be grateful for them. Don't think there's much to be grateful about? How about these for starters: a roof over your head, clean water to drink, enough food to eat, the loving relationships in your life, a free education, a relatively safe and stable place to live.

I've been to enough war zones and places of desperate poverty to not take these things for granted any more. Now I'm so grateful for all the advantages and opportunities I've had throughout my life, and I believe all of us have something to be grateful for.

It's about an attitude of gratitude

Why not see how far your kindness can go? You'll be amazed at the positive impact you can have on the people around you, and how it can come back to you when you least expect it.

Everyday Adventure #8

You may not be in a position to make national news or raise thousands of pounds, but there are loads of ways you can pay your gratitude forward and spread joy in your community and beyond.

It could be as simple as leaving a book you've just read and enjoyed at a bus stop for someone else to find, maybe with a note to ask that whoever finds it does the same when they're finished. Maybe you could do that with this book?

If you're aiming big, the most inspiring stories (as you might have been taught in your English lessons) start with planning the who, what, when, where and why. Let's give that a go:

Who?

Start with thinking about who you want to reach with your kindness. Is it an individual or a group? It might be someone you already know, or a complete stranger. It could be a charity who are looking for volunteers, or an older person who lives nearby and doesn't seem to get out of their house much.

What?

Next, you need to think about what you could do for them.

It could be something where you roll your sleeves up and get stuck straight in, like joining a litter pick, helping out at a local festival, or volunteering at a community event. Or it might be taking part in something that raises funds or awareness for a particular cause, perhaps a sponsored bike ride, or a peaceful climate change protest.

When?

When you make a commitment to do something, you need to know that you can follow it through. Whether it's doing something little and often or dedicating larger chunks of time every few months, perhaps in the school holidays, do it in a way you can realistically stick to. Don't be a flake.

Where?

The obvious place to start is somewhere you know well, perhaps your school, a local village or town. But there's no reason you can't set a goal to go further afield, there are no limits when it comes to spreading kindness.

Why?

As we covered earlier, it's important to think about that end goal – the reason you're doing what you're doing.

Now, this shouldn't be your main motivation, but there are plenty of benefits for you from selfless commitment:

- A sense of satisfaction

- Self-worth
- New friendships and connections
- Confidence
- Gaining new skills
- Great for your CV, uni or college application!

Tips
- Start small
- Follow your own interests
- Don't over-commit – with your time, money or energy (remember your Priority Pyramid!)

Checkpoint

If you've been paying attention, you'll know that **selfless commitment** is the last of my values and arguably my most motivating. In times where I can't muster the energy to do something for myself, I can always find it for someone else. Does that sound like you, too? Here's some more inspiration.

- **Service**: a willingness to help and contribute to the well-being of others.
- **Generosity**: providing support and resources without expecting anything in return.
- **Compassion**: demonstrating empathy and concern for the needs of others.

- **Duty**: fulfilling responsibilities and obligations with a strong sense of commitment.
- **Empathy**: understanding and sharing the feelings and experiences of others.
- **Kindness**: treating others with consideration, care and goodwill.
- **Humanitarianism**: advocating for the welfare and dignity of all people.
- **Care**: expressing concern and providing support for the well-being of others.
- **Social responsibility**: recognising and addressing societal needs and challenges.

INSPIRE TO ACHIEVE

'The most dangerous thing you can do is to follow the crowd. The crowd is often wrong, misled, or manipulated. The crowd is not you, it does not know your goals, your values, or your potential. The crowd is not your leader, your mentor, or your friend. Be yourself, not the crowd.'

SCOTT D. CLARY

'Inspire to Achieve' is the motto of the Army Cadet Force, and I'm truly honoured to be their national ambassador. The ACF strives to encourage its members to develop their potential, to have pride in themselves and respect for each other. They instil the values and standards I've talked about throughout this book through a programme of exciting and challenging activities such as fieldcraft, adventure training, first aid, music and sports, to name a few. If this sounds like something you'd like to get involved in, there's a link in the 'Resources' section at the end of this book where you can find out more.

But what if you don't think the cadets are for you?

In that case, you'll have to...

CHOOSE YOUR OWN ADVENTURE

As you've worked your way through this book you've completed a series of **Everyday Adventures**. You didn't need a passport, you've not got any special equipment, and you've probably not got a phone full of social media-worthy photos to show for it. But I promise you, you've just conquered something.

You might be thinking, 'Alright, Jord, you've really lost the plot now.' But for me, adventure is not just a one-time experience, a fleeting moment of excitement or an expedition to a remote location on the other side of the world. It's a way of approaching life and a way of thinking.

Adventure can be big or small, but take it from me, you'll get just as much satisfaction from the seemingly unremarkable ones as you would from the death-defying, headline-grabbing escapades.

It could be as simple as joining a new club, talking to an older person in your family about their life experiences or just getting out in nature. Embracing adventure means constantly seeking new challenges, stepping outside your comfort zone and approaching life with an open and curious mind.

Choosing adventure as a way of life is like looking at the

world as a playground filled with possibilities. We learn to embrace challenges as opportunities for growth rather than fearing the unknown. This mindset allows us to adapt and thrive in the face of adversity, knowing that every obstacle is a chance to learn, evolve and emerge stronger.

That all leads us to a more fulfilling and meaningful existence. It keeps us engaged, excited and motivated to create a life that aligns with our goals and values. We find joy in the little things and push ourselves beyond what we once thought possible.

BE THE DIFFERENCE THAT MAKES THE DIFFERENCE

How do you feel about your future? If someone had asked me that question at fifteen, as I sat in that sad little jail cell in Blackpool, I'm not sure I could've even made up an answer. I certainly couldn't have imagined the life I've gone on to live.

I've no doubt that my values have turned my life around, perhaps – at times – even saved it.

From the kid who hated school to the man who built a school. From someone who couldn't imagine life beyond my hometown, to adventures in every corner of the globe, across all seven continents. From disappointing every teacher, youth worker and well-meaning grown up who tried to help me, to receiving an honour from His Majesty the King.

It's not easy to achieve all the dreams and goals you set for yourself, but it's a darn sight easier when you find your inspiration – your *why*. Once you find that, everything else becomes easier.

To live a life guided by values is to value yourself. So, guided by your values, when opportunity comes knocking at your door, don't just crack it open an inch or two. Kick that door clean off its bloody hinges!

You don't need to have a crystal-clear vision of your future. Who actually gives a jot about a five-year plan? But by knowing your values, and living your life by those values, you now have a compass for your journey. They'll show you the way when you ask them and set you on the right course if you find yourself lost.

With them, you'll go out into the world a happier, more resilient person.

The hard work doesn't stop here. You'll need to constantly challenge yourself, challenge your values. Push yourself to your absolute limits. But always remember:

Your greatest adventure is becoming who you are.

Wherever you go, and however you get there, I wish you the best of luck.

ACKNOWLEDGEMENTS

First and foremost, I would like to express my deepest gratitude to my dear friend Joanna Mitchell Hynes. Your encouragement and support helped me bring this passion project, which has lived in my heart for so many years, to life. I am forever thankful for your belief in me, even when I struggled to believe in myself.

A heartfelt thank you to James Stephens, publisher at Biteback Publishing, and all members of his team. Your faith in this project and your commitment to helping me get this book into the hands of as many young people as possible has been nothing short of inspiring. Thank you for giving me a platform once again to share my work with the world.

To my family: your love, patience and unwavering support have been the foundation that carried me through this journey and so many others. I owe everything to your constant encouragement, and I am forever grateful.

I also want to thank all the young people I've had the privilege of meeting over the past seven years as national ambassador for the Army Cadet Force. You are the reason for this book. Your energy, curiosity and hunger for growth inspire me daily. To the adult volunteers who dedicate their lives to guiding the next generation, thank you for your selfless commitment. You are changing the world, one life at a time.

Finally, to anyone I may have unintentionally hurt or let down on my own journey, I offer my sincere apologies. You have taught me invaluable lessons, and I genuinely and wholeheartedly wish you nothing but peace and positivity always.

Thank you to everyone who has been a part of this process. This book exists because of you.

RESOURCES

Watch

You can find videos of me talking about various subjects on my website: **jordanwylie.org/speaking**

TED Talks

Be inspired by scientists, musicians, innovators and activists – all under the age of twenty: **ted.com/playlists/129**

Army Cadets UK

There's loads of inspiring content from the cadets over on their YouTube channel: **youtube.com/@ArmyCadetsUK**

Listen

'The Socially Awkward' podcast is something to remind you that you're not the only one walking around this planet feeling, well, awkward.

The podcast 'Mostly Mindful for Teens and Tweens' offers quick mindfulness practices to build resiliency.

'This Teenage Life' is a teen-led podcast that offers advice on relatable issues.

Talk
There's always someone on the other end of a phone you can talk to. The following phone lines are completely free:

Childline: **0800 1111**
Samaritans: **116 123**
Young Minds: Text **YM** to **85258** for 24-hour urgent care.

If you're dealing with something that's particularly challenging or persistent, you might want to consider involving a mental health professional.

Read
Author Nicola Morgan has written a whole heap of amazing advice, all aimed at young people: nicolamorgan.com

Join
armycadets.com

Are you feeling inspired by Jordan?

Why not do something amazing and raise money for ACCT UK, the official charity for Army Cadets UK?

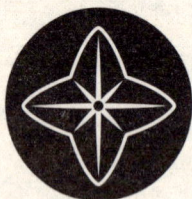

Army Cadet Charitable Trust UK

acctuk.org/fundraise

Our values are...

A - Abiding
We learn from the past and plan for the future.

C - Committed
We are dedicated in our mission to empower young people through Army Cadets activities and inspire them to achieve.

C -Courageous
We believe in aiming higher and supporting all young people to access life-changing opportunities

T - Trustworthy
We are inclusive and principled. We want young people to accept one another for who they are and build positive relationships.